In Contempt

"What's he been doin'?"

"Overthrowin' the guvment."

IN CONTEMPT

Defending Free Speech, Defeating HUAC

Ed Yellin and Jean Fagan Yellin

University of Michigan Press

Ann Arbor

Published in the United States of America by the
University of Michigan Press
Manufactured in the United States of America
Printed on acid-free paper
First published January 2022

A CIP catalog record for this book is available from the British Library.

Library of Congress Cataloging-in-Publication data has been applied for.

ISBN 978-0-472-03891-6 (paper : alk. paper)
ISBN 978-0-472-90264-4 (OA)

DOI: https://doi.org/10.3998/mpub.12182796

Political Cartoon by Art Young, courtesy of the University of Michigan Library
(Joseph A. Labadie Collection, Special Collections Research Center)

Linocuts by Jean Yellin, created as greeting cards during the years of the Yellin
case, inspired by Pablo Picasso's famous 1949 image of a peace dove.

In loving memory of Peter, and to Lisa and Michael

Also to Mosé, Benjamin, Sarah, Blaze,

And to Simon, Isa, Nico, Miles, Madison, Lucienne, and Declan

Huge thanks to Lisa and Michael

Special thanks to Esther Cohen and Lawrence Bush

Let your life be a counter friction to stop the machine.

—"CIVIL DISOBEDIENCE," HENRY DAVID THOREAU

TABLE OF CONTENTS

Digital materials related to this title can be found on the Fulcrum platform via the following citable URL https://doi.org/10.3998/mpub.12182796

FOREWORD

I was a newborn when my parents and grandmother bought a house together in 1952 in St. Albans, Queens, a New York neighborhood that was being deserted by its white residents. My parents, along with five other couples—all of them white, Jewish, and Communist Party activists—plunged their meager savings into St. Albans houses in hope of keeping the neighborhood integrated.

Four years later, when my older brother's second-grade class photo came home from school, he and the teacher were the only white faces on display.

There were many such failures and even follies associated with being a Communist in America—most horrifically, the movement's blindness to the murderous nature of the Soviet system—yet in my estimation, as a red-diaper baby and as a writer and editor with a strong historical sensibility, the Communists of my parents' and grandmother's generations were among the brightest, most courageous, most idealistic, and most self-sacrificing citizens this country has known. They never numbered more than 100,000— of whom nearly a third were nonreligious Jews—and their cohort fell precipitously during the years described in Ed and Jean Yellin's *In Contempt*. Yet without their dogged activism, the United States might never have seen unionization in hospitals, steel mills, textile and garment factories, hotels and restaurants, or on the docks of the West Coast. Many aspects of Franklin Delano Roosevelt's New Deal, including Social Security, might never have been legislated had FDR not felt the pressure of the Communist movement's agitation among workers.

Folks like my parents and grandmother were also far ahead of their time in strenuously opposing racial segregation, Jim Crow laws, the racial terrorism of lynching, and other grim legacies of American slavery. They were committed to breaking with the racist consensus of white America, in the lives they led, the culture they created (popular music, jazz, folk music, literature, film, and more), and the relationships and values they cultivated.

Their outsized influence, which peaked during the U.S.-USSR wartime alliance against Nazism, attracted the repressive apparatus of the U.S. government immediately after the war. McCarthyism actually rose up in the 1940s, years before Wisconsin Republican senator Joseph McCarthy even stepped before the newfangled television cameras, and Communists and their allies (as well as lots and lots of gay people and Jews) were soon being harassed out of the fields of education, entertainment, labor organizing, scientific research, government, and more.

The legal ordeal described in *In Contempt* began with a subpoena from the House of Representatives' Committee on (so-called) Un-American Activities, known as HUAC. For my family, McCarthyism invaded more gently: when I was eight years old, home alone with my brother, two FBI agents paid a visit. They said they were looking for my grandmother, who had been a member of the Communist Party since its founding in 1921–22. When my parents came home from work that day and heard about that visit, they sat my brother and me down for a serious conversation, and my world shifted.

My folks had already left the CP, however, as thousands of others did in the late 1950s, after Nikita Khrushchev denounced his predecessor, Joseph Stalin, and they finally grasped the reality of the "dictatorship of the proletariat." As for my grandmother, she had gone "underground" by taking a live-in position at a nursing home on Long Island. So while the FBI agents certainly left an impression on me, they represented little ongoing threat to my family. Not so for the Yellins and their three young kids, who would endure several years of economic hardship and constant worry as to whether Ed would end up in a federal prison. All this thanks to his refusal to answer questions about his political affiliations and beliefs, based on his own deep devotion to the First Amendment.

Happily, Ed and Jean Yellin have outlived HUAC by more than half a century. While concerns about free speech and government repression remain very much with us in Trump-time, *In Contempt* is less a warning than a testament to the enduring quality of patriotic dissent in our evolving democracy—and a loving reconstruction of what it meant to be labeled "un-American" for defending the Constitution.

—Lawrence Bush
Editor emeritus, *Jewish Currents*
Author of *BESSIE: A Novel of Love and Revolution*

Introduction

RED DIAPERS

ED

I was born in 1927, three and a half years after my sister, Esther, into a nonobservant Jewish working-class family. My folks, Sarah and Alex (his Yiddish name was Hillel), emigrated from Belarus in 1921. Daddy was thirty-one and Mom was twenty-six. They didn't talk much to us kids about the "old country," but some things I do remember. Momma was very proud of her older brother, Sam, who participated in the 1905 Revolution and then joined the Bolsheviks to overthrow the czar and form the world's first socialist government in 1917. When the family came to America, Mom her younger sister Jenny, her older brother Sam, and her younger brother Harry all became part of the Jewish, socialist, working-class movement in New York that later formed the American Communist Party. They were all part of a rising union movement among plumbers, garment workers, retail workers, and others. At that time, the Communist Party worked closely with other leftwing groups in building this union movement.

My birthplace was Brooklyn, but when the Depression hit us in 1932 we moved to the South Bronx to live in an apartment with Jenny, whose husband, Jack, was a master plumber and assured of work. Harry and Bevy, their children, were a few years older than my older sister Esther. I think we were there for about a year before our family's finances improved and we found our own apartment in the same building. (I'd like to be able to say I was "born and bred in 'Da Bronx,'" but I can't.)

In 1935, when I was eight, I took the subway down to Union Square with my family and friends for May Day, the international workers' holiday, while Esther, at eleven, was old enough to ride the subway with her Young Pioneer friends, wearing their white blouses and red kerchiefs, the symbol of the Communist left. When she returned that evening, she cried to Momma that she had been hassled on the subway for being a "dirty red." Momma shouted, "That's it! We're moving to the Coops!"

Pronounced as in "chicken coops," not "co-ops," short for Workers Cooperative Colony, the Coops were a housing complex in the northeast Bronx across the street from Bronx Park. That's where Esther and I began to identify as real "red-diaper babies," and where this memoir really begins, because that upbringing strongly influenced—one might even say, determined—the choices I made in the years of the "Yellin Case."

Built as a cooperative, arguably the first cooperative housing project in New York City, the Coops consisted of 750 apartments covering two blocks. The buildings were four stories high, with no elevators, and divided into sections, with only three or four apartments per floor. This design allowed for open courtyards and "cross-ventilation" in each bedroom. In contrast to buildings with long hallways and multiple apartments on each floor, there was a sense of intimacy among neighbors. A basement contained a cafeteria, freeing mothers and, in some cases, fathers, too, to come home late from work or meetings and trust that their children would be adequately fed. Also in the basement were a large library with mostly Yiddish books; an auditorium for meetings, lectures, concerts, and dances; a food market; an office for a social director provided by the city; rooms for a secular Yiddish *shule* (school), where reading, writing, and speaking were taught (everything in the context of leftwing politics); and, very important for adolescent youngsters, clubrooms where we could dance, schmooze, woo, and form clubs for organized activities: photography, woodshop, weight lifting, and more. There were so many children in the Coops that we could self-organize by age into social and athletic clubs. The age range was usually only two years per club!

The organizers and members of the board of directors in this unique environment were overwhelmingly leftwing secular Jews: Socialists, Trotskyists, and, in the majority, Communists. Not all were affiliated, but most were sympathetic. We sent large contingents and an award-winning IWO (International Workers Order) Bugle and Drum Corps to the May Day parades. If that holiday fell on a school day, we skipped school, with our parents' permission. When we marched, we sang songs of protest: against racism and anti-Semitism; for trade unionism; for a socialist world in which all people, workers and farmers, would be equal, with no rich and no poor; and for an end to war!

In the Bronx and beyond we were known as "Little Moscow." It was an absolutely wonderful environment in which to grow up. As I write this, eighty years after moving to the Coops, I am still in touch with my few living friends and comrades. We shared an overwhelming sense of togetherness and belonging—not just to any group but to a movement with high ideals, an oppressed movement that struggled for human rights the world over!

Within our family there were frequent house parties: *freylekh* (joyous) events with singing—Yiddish and Russian folk songs and leftwing songs, accompanied by cousin Ely's *khamoshke* (concertina) and fueled by a bit of *schnaps* (sweet brandy, often homemade). In later years, as veterans of various youth groups, Jean and I would replicate such parties as both private and public hootenannies. Nurtured on union songs and folk songs, we not only had enjoyed concerts in the Coops auditorium but in the larger hall on Allerton Avenue. Long before most Americans had heard of Woody Guthrie, Pete Seeger, Leadbelly (Huddie Ledbetter), Cisco Houston, and the Almanac Singers, we Young Communists had heard them and sung with them in our neighborhood!

Here are some remembrances that trigger the spirit of growing up in the Coops: shining shoes for 10¢ (more if the customer was generous) to raise money in support of the Lincoln Brigade, the American volunteers who fought against Francisco Franco's fascists in the Spanish Civil War; going to the subway yards with my mother and her comrades to leaflet the workers, urging them to join the Transport Workers Union; being recruited, as a high school student at Stuyvesant, to picket a nonunion barbershop, from which I single-handedly kept out almost all the patrons. (I found out later that it was a mob-run union, but I did learn that I could be an effective picketer.) I also remember climbing a ladder at the Allerton Avenue subway station to address people coming home from work. Although I can't recall the topic or the audience's size or response, I do remember my knees shaking uncontrollably as I climbed that ladder. Most of all, I remember the spirit and comradery of May Day and the bonds that formed among us Coop-niks.

The streets and apartments were hot in the summer, and it was expensive to send us to camp or go to a resort in the Catskills, so in 1938 my folks managed to buy a plot of land in the Goldens Bridge Cooperative Colony (GB) in upper Westchester County. Advertised "For Workers and Professionals Only," it was one of many summer colonies organized by the left. GB was the Coops all over again. Building our GB house was a truly cooperative effort, with framing by a close family friend, plumbing by Uncles Jack and Harry, electricity by cousin Paul, and painting by everyone. The work was done in three stages. First year: no ceiling and only one side of each wall covered; kerosene lamps and stove; outdoor shower (cold water); a classic outhouse. Second year: electricity. Third year: indoor plumbing (although we were encouraged to use the outhouse so as not to overload the septic tank). The inside walls and ceiling came slowly, over time. "Good enough for who it's for" was our motto.

The Colony had a camp for children from nursery school to teenagers, and a barn that served as an auditorium, where we folk danced, heard lectures and music, staged our own plays and skits, and danced every Saturday night. I spent part or all of eleven summers, from 1938 to 1948, in GB. In '43, at sixteen, I was a junior lifeguard. In '44, '45 and '46, I bussed and waited on tables in the Catskills and Poconos for most of the summer, but the rest was spent in GB. In the fall of '45, I was drafted into the U.S. Navy but was discharged in time to be in GB for a few summer weeks.

I was an engineering student at CCNY from the fall of '46 to January '48, when I transferred to the University of Michigan. Still I spent the summer of '48 working as a busboy in the Catskills, but that only lasted about two weeks. At the end of the second week, the manager of the resort, the Napanoch Country Club, called the dining room staff together and announced that he was having financial problems and we would be compelled to work only for tips. Under New York State labor law, busboys were to be paid $7.50 per week. If we wished to remain on the job, we were told, we would have to endorse our checks over to the country club on Friday, payday. This was intolerable! No self-respecting member of the working class would work under those conditions, and we gathered in our bunkhouse and decided that on Friday we would refuse to return our checks. If we all stood together we could beat the bosses! The decision was unanimous: We'd whip their asses! But on Friday, I was the only one who refused to turn over my $7.50.

Handed my walking papers, I hitchhiked to Cleveland and camped out on the porch of the girls' boarding house where Jean, whom I'd met at the University of Michigan, was living while studying at the Cleveland Art Institute. The rest is history! Five months later Jean and I would be married in Ann Arbor.

After my few days in Cleveland, I hitched rides back to Goldens Bridge and spent the rest of the summer in heaven. If the Coops weren't enough to make me a red-diaper baby, surely GB finished the job.

It's amazing how influential were those thirteen years in the Coops, mixed with eleven in Goldens Bridge, along with my mother's milk, in shaping the circumstances and decisions of my later life including my decision to become a colonizer, a steelworker in Gary, Indiana, for eight years.

What was the Communist Party's policy of colonization all about? And how did the House Un-American Activities Committee (HUAC) interpret that policy? How did I see my own role as a colonizer? In chapter 1, 1 discuss the hearing to which HUAC subjected me and introduce sections of the transcript of that hearing—in particular, comments by HUAC members dealing with colonization and the testimony of John Lautner, a perennial anti-Communist "expert" witness who testified that colonization was a conspiracy. By definition, a conspiracy is a plot to break the law. In my experience, however—and I have spoken to many friends and acquaintances who agree—

neither we nor the Communist Party "conspired" when we chose to seek employment in various industries.

Briefly, very briefly, Marxist thinking held that the working class, in particular those in basic industry (steel, mining, manufacturing, transportation, and so forth), would organize into unions and provide the force for transitioning into a more equitable socialist society. Communist Party policy was to support and to participate in unionization. Party members became organizers and made important contributions, particularly to the growth of the CIO (Congress of Industrial Organizations), founded in 1935. For various reasons, after World War II the Party lost its support among the working class and developed a policy of asking some of its younger members to seek jobs and become organizers in basic industry. Those who were approached usually were mobile, young, not yet settled into family life, and dedicated to working for a more equitable society.

There were as many reasons for choosing to join the working class as there were recruits. I really had no leadership abilities, I just wanted to be a worker. If you think I was an idiot and that colonization was a stupid policy, you are correct. If the Party couldn't find adherents among the working class, they should have figured out why and either changed their policies or waited for more opportune times! My mother, a loyal and dedicated Communist, put it to me bluntly: "Show me a single leader of the Party who has sent his son to work in a factory!" Did I listen to her? No! Am I sorry I quit college in 1948 and found a job in the Gary, Indiana Big Mill of U.S. Steel? Yes! But do I regret spending eight years of my life working in the open hearth? No! No regrets! It was a learning experience and I am not sorry.

If I hadn't been a colonizer, I would have had eight more years as a scientist, which would have been much more rewarding than shoveling dolomite into a stinking, hot furnace, or shoveling manganese and other alloys into a boiling cauldron of steel. But it was a life experience I would not otherwise have had, and who knows what I would have missed by not living and working in Gary? Jean and I made lifelong friends there with folks we would not have found in academia.

Of course, we would not have gone through the five years of "the case," but that too was an important life experience—and we survived it, arguably stronger than ever!

Another factor should be considered in the discussion of why I quit college and went to work in Gary. It's a digression, but it does make me appear less of a fool in choosing to quit college before getting my degree.

In 1944, when I reached seventeen, I took an exam administered by the U.S. Navy to test my ability to become a radio technician. I passed the exam and was eligible to enlist, but to my great surprise, I failed the physical because I was red-green color blind. How could I become a radio technician or a sailor if I were color blind? The irony is that when I turned eighteen and was subjected to the draft, I passed the regular physical, which did not include the color-blind test. At desk number one, the clerk saw I had passed the physical and stamped "Navy." At desk number two, the clerk said, "You can't be in the navy, you're color blind! Oh well, it's already stamped, so go to the navy line."

I like to think that upon hearing the news that I was to be inducted into the armed forces, Japan surrendered the next day. Technically, however, the war didn't officially end until a year later. I did my time in boot camp and then was sent to Washington, D.C. to take a desk job in the Navy Bureau of Personnel, replacing a WAVE (Women Accepted for Voluntary Emergency Service) so she could be discharged and return home. After only ten months of service, I, too, was discharged. Eligible for the G.I. Bill, I returned to the City College of New York, where I took the tough prerequisites for mechanical engineering—calculus, physics, mathematics, differential equations—as well as required courses in the liberal arts. I worked hard and did okay, but not up to my usual standards. Somehow I had lost my drive; the thrill of solving problems in the sciences and mathematics was gone. What to do?

Because I had a year left on the G.I. Bill, I took the big step of leaving CCNY and my hometown. I enrolled in the University of Michigan, which was reputed to have a first-class engineering school. From then on, it was all downhill! Compared to CCNY, Michigan was a breeze. Students did what was unheard of back

East: They went to the movies in the middle of the week. They even cut classes and played cards. (I won a hundred dollars one afternoon, bought a bike, and found it stolen the next day because I was ashamed to lock it up, thinking that the onlookers would find me to be a terrible person because I didn't trust them.)

With my drive to succeed academically lost, after the first semester I transferred to mathematics. That didn't help, and as proof that I was in trouble, I next became a psychology major! Approached by a Communist Party member to "go into industry," I was more than ready. No persuasion was needed. Given a choice of getting a job in an auto plant or in a steel mill, I chose the mill, and with Jean's agreement we set off for Gary, Indiana, to start a new life. When my mother declared, "Show me a Party functionary who has sent his son to work in a factory," I responded with a letter expressing shock that she could want me to become a professor.

That provides some of the background for my decision to defy HUAC and, in particular, to assert my rights to free speech and assembly. This book is not the place to discuss the terrible things done by world Communism, in particular by the Soviet Union. It's enough to say that I remain a communist, but with a small "c"! At this writing, I might even describe myself as a democratic socialist.

JEAN

I was born in 1930, the fourth daughter in a radical Midwestern newspaper family. My father, Peter, the atheistic oldest son of a birthright Quaker and a devout Irish Catholic, upset his mother when he became not a priest but a Marxist journalist. My mother, Sarah, the first of four Orthodox Jewish daughters who were, of course, not encouraged to study (unlike their older brother), became a University of Michigan Phi Beta Kappa, a teacher, and a socialist activist. Peter's family, which in this country reached back to the sixteenth century, had gone west to Michigan before the territory became a state, and built homesteads at what is now called Holly. Raised on the farm, Peter liked to live near trees, but because he was working in Lansing as a reporter covering state politics for the Detroit dailies, Peter and Sarah lived in East Lansing. This was, I think, a disastrous choice for their children: we were pariahs in the town not only because our mother was Jewish and our parents leftists, but because they voiced their radical ideas weekly by publishing a pro-labor newspaper.

Fortunately, the four of us—Ruth, Mary, Ann, and I—had each other. And we had books.

When I was very young, my father told me the cautionary tale of a little girl who decided to read a book in the Library of Congress each day, and who died, an old woman, in the middle of the letter C. He wasn't opposing literacy, just trying to convince me that I couldn't read *everything*.

I was four when my parents began to publish the *News of Lansing*. In the 1930s, the struggle to organize the autoworkers was crucial, and I knew that both my mother and my father were directly involved in the birth of the United Auto Workers Union.

I must have been seven when, aware that my parents had hidden a group of photos behind the tall bookcase so that I couldn't see them, I climbed up to look. I discovered a stack of pictures printed on strange slick paper and smelling odd. They had been sent by the Spanish government to American newspapers to rally support for the Republican cause after the bombing of Guernica, the first civilian slaughter perpetrated by German and Italian planes attacking Republican Spain during the run-up to World War II. I saw a little girl like me crying amid rubble, and for a week I had nightmares. Today, I can still see her.

In June 1937, I heard about the Lansing Labor Holiday, when union men, whose wives had been arrested at night while looking for them, drove their jalopies into the streets to block traffic and shut down the state capital. That was the day Lansing became a union town. The *News of Lansing* was one of the few businesses permitted to remain open. Late in the afternoon, a group of emboldened workers walked the four miles to East Lansing and were met by hostile Reserve Officers' Training Corps (ROTC) college boys who angrily dunked them in the Red Cedar River, which ran through campus.

A few years later, I was in our living room when a group of pacifist students who had been similarly attacked by ROTC boys and pushed into that river appeared at our house dripping wet and shivering, followed by a mob coming up the street. Mother quickly found blankets for the boys, then shooed away newsmen who appeared at our door asking where the students could be found. She stared them down, saying, "Do you think I'd let them in here? My children are at home."

Mostly I got my political education by assiduously reading newspapers and listening and contributing to the conversations at the dinner table every night. Ours was a family in which ideas were respected, even when voiced by me, its youngest member. I have a clear recollection of speaking up during some political discussion and shocking our guests, who apparently had never before seen a young child permitted into an adult conversation. I became politically involved at seventeen, after my father's death, when I enrolled at the University of Michigan at Ann Arbor and moved into student co-ops (as had my sister Ann), and began writing for the student paper, the *Michigan Daily*. Also, as a matter of course, I joined the Ralph Neafus Club of the Communist Party. It was the only game in town. As I recall, meetings were not particularly interesting, and I don't remember any actions we were involved in—but I do remember meeting the comrades, including Ed Yellin, and I did relish the feeling, after so many years of isolation in East Lansing, that I was part of a worldwide movement for social change.

My role in our decision to move to Gary, I am distressed to report, was essentially passive. I was tired of being in school and, now married and amazingly blind to the issue of sexism, envisioned my future as the mother of children. In addition, foolishly ignoring the reality of class in America, I thought it wouldn't make much difference to me and our future babies whether Ed worked in a steel mill or at some other sort of job. My only excuse is that I was just eighteen!

It was in Gary that I began to experience sexism, classism, and racism, and where I birthed my three children, Peter, Lisa, and Michael. In terms of my own career development, those were eight lost years, but in terms of learning how to live, they were precious.

By the time Ed and I decided to leave Gary, I felt that I could have stayed there forever.

Having Ed called before HUAC was not really a shock. My father, known as a leftist journalist, had been named before HUAC long after his death, and we had friends who had been subpoenaed, which I took as a badge of merit. Asserting the First Amendment seemed to me a fine idea; I had grown up in a family committed to freedom of speech and of the press. Of course, Ed's trial, conviction, and sentencing to jail was another story, but I didn't believe he would have to serve time. What I did know was that my years growing up in East Lansing had taught me to ignore what people and the press said. I had learned to keep my mouth closed if I didn't want to be quoted. I was practically immune to public disapproval. Melt into a community? I knew how. Live on little? I had done it. Go to school? I was good at that, and it was to prove my salvation.

One morning in 1960, a generation later, after Ed had been sentenced to a year in jail for contempt of Congress, I escaped the kids and the house and headed for the dime store. At the school supplies counter, I looked at the notebooks and diaries long and hard. I knew that we were into something big, and I knew that I should be keeping a log so I could write about it some day. But staring at the record books, I decided NO. I simply could not write down what was happening in our lives each day. It was hard enough to live it; it would be too hard to record it, too.

A lifetime later, we are reporting on the "Yellin Case." Our story now has not only a beginning, but also a middle and an end. From this distance of decades, we now know much of what happened and why. And we have learned important lessons—above all, about what political freedom means and requires in this country. Unfortunately, these lessons are once again of pressing relevance. Many political commenters have noted the parallels between the current political climate and McCarthyism. Our story needs to be told, as much as we need to tell it.

There are, of course, a number of excellent books about McCarthyism, from Victor Navasky's *Naming Names* to Ellen Schrecker's *Many Are the Crimes*. What sets our story apart is its focus on how a family coped with a series of attacks during the McCarthy period, and how we managed to survive. The persecution of one man who was a husband and father had effects that ricocheted across generations of our family. As the oldest child, Peter had the clearest recollections. Our book illuminates how injustice is rarely, if ever, visited upon one person alone.

A story of how people stand up to oppression always matters, but it matters particularly today, when "national security" is again being pitted against the people's rights to privacy, freedom of speech, and freedom of association. We think that, while seniors like ourselves may be interested in remembering life in the 1950s and '60s, young people should also take note. They may have heard a little in school about the McCarthyite repression, but a story like ours will allow them to connect their feelings of alienation from their government to an earlier struggle.

What follows are our recollections of the five years of the "Yellin Case." Admittedly, we are offering more of a historical chronology than an expression of our personal feelings—for we had to steel ourselves, not let our emotions take over, to create a safe place for our family. Instead, we trusted in the First Amendment of the Constitution of the United States of America, and that trust was ultimately rewarded.

Sarasota, Florida
September 2019

CHAPTER ONE

A Knock at the Door

ED

It was another one of those 300 days of bright sunshine in Fort Collins, Colorado, where I was enrolled as a mechanical engineering junior at Colorado State University. Although it was late in January 1958, with the midmorning temperature at around 15°, the air was so dry that it felt well above freezing. Then came the proverbial knock on the door, and John Wayne appeared in a ten-gallon Stetson and gray Western-style suit. Actually, in that outfit and at six feet tall he only looked to be John Wayne, which I realized when he tipped the brim of his hat and said, "Excuse me, I'm a marshal come up from Denver, and I'm sorry to have to present you with this subpoena."

I took it, Jean put down her coffee, and the marshal rode off into the sunset. The subpoena stated:

UNITED STATES OF AMERICA Congress of the United States

To . . . Edward Yellin, 150 Woodland, Fort Collins, Colorado

GREETING:

Pursuant to lawful authority, YOU ARE HEREBY COMMANDED

to be and appear before the Committee on Un-American Activities of the House of Representatives of the United States, or a duly appointed subcommittee thereof, on February 10 (Monday), 1958, at ten o'clock a.m. at City Council Chambers, City Hall, Gary, Indiana then and there to testify touching matters of inquiry committed to said committee, and not to depart without leave of said committee.

HEREOF FAIL NOT, as you will answer your default under the pains and penalties in such cases made and provided.

To . . . U.S. Marshal . . . to serve and return.

GIVEN under my hand this . . . 21 . . . day of . . . January . . . in this year of our Lord, 1958.

(Signed) Francis E. Walter, Chairman

Chairman of Subcommittee-Member Designate of the Committee on Un-American Activities of the House of Representatives.

February 10, 1958.

WOW!

The subpoena didn't state the title/purpose of the hearing, but a quick call to a friend in Gary found it in the local newspaper: "INVESTIGATION OF COMMUNIST INFILTRATION AND PROPAGANDA ACTIVITIES IN BASIC INDUSTRY (GARY, IND., AREA)."

We, of course, knew of the many hearings conducted by HUAC, the House Un-American Activities Committee, particularly of the Hollywood Ten, a group of prominent Hollywood writers, actors, and directors summoned to appear before HUAC in 1947. Arguing that their First Amendment rights to freedom of speech and association were being violated, they denounced the Committee's investigation of Communist influence in the film industry. Convicted of contempt of Congress and subsequently blacklisted, the Hollywood Ten variously served between six months and a year in jail, and the whole world knew that they had been banned from working for the major film studios, a blacklisting that would not end until the 1960s. Maybe I shouldn't have been surprised at being summoned to yet another HUAC investigation of "subversive activities." After all, I had been a member of the Communist Party, and, even though Senator Joseph McCarthy had been discredited and had died some three years earlier, McCarthyism lived on, stoked by the Cold War. When, in a wrongheaded effort to strengthen its presence among the working class, the Party had adopted a policy of colonization, urging members to leave school and find work in basic industry, I had agreed to find work in a Gary, Indiana, steel mill. HUAC had held hearings in many cities, including the industrial centers of Detroit, Flint, and Buffalo, so why not in Gary? After all, six months after we left Gary and I returned to college to finish my degree, we were not thinking about the past. When Sputnik, the first artificial earth satellite, was launched by the Soviet Union in October 1957, I recall walking across campus to the engineering building while looking up at the blue sky and telling myself, "Now I can get a PhD. Money will be pouring into the sciences to catch up to the Soviets. We can't let them beat us to outer space!"

Here in the foothills of the Rockies, Jean and I hadn't thought McCarthyism would reach us. Think again! That subpoena was the beginning of the five years of the "Yellin Case"—years of victory and defeat, reward and loss, anxiety and elation, struggle, and yet more struggle!

JEAN

One of the first things we did was call my sister Ann. How wonderful to have a constitutional lawyer in the family! This phone call resulted in a sheaf of closely argued single spaced letters outlining our legal situation. It also resulted in our retaining her friend Victor Rabinowitz of the New York firm of Rabinowitz and Boudin. Vic was a well-known progressive civil liberties lawyer who had represented many witnesses before congressional committees and many defendants before district and appellate courts, as well as before the Supreme Court.

There was no way to avoid responding to the subpoena. Our question was simply how to respond to HUAC's questions? Together with Ann, Vic gave us a crash course in HUAC.

In the decade since they'd sent the Hollywood Ten to jail, HUAC had been riding high. By 1950, a witness called before a congressional committee investigating the Communist Party had five options. First, admit Communist Party membership, name others as Communists—thereby guaranteeing that they would be called before the Committee—and go home free. Second, refuse to comply by pleading the Fifth Amendment, claiming that one's answers would be self-incriminating, and go home free but branded by the press as "a Fifth Amendment Communist," likely losing your job because of the publicity. Third, deny Communist Party membership and risk a perjury indictment based on the corrupt testimony of HUAC's paid anticommunist witnesses. Fourth, admit Communist Party membership and refuse to name others, thereby risking indictment. Fifth, refuse to comply by pleading the First Amendment—freedom of speech and association—and, with a good lawyer and a sympathetic judge, trust to luck.

ED

We went with luck. We all agreed that it would be unthinkable to cooperate with any congressional committee investigating the so-called Communist conspiracy or any activities related to ideas, speech, or assembly. These were rights protected by the First Amendment to the Constitution. Because Congress cannot enact laws restricting these rights, it cannot investigate in these areas. The history of HUAC investigations was clear: The Committee was interested in creating a climate of fear that fueled Cold War policies and suppressed voices that opposed those policies. Intimidation, not legislation, was their goal.

I had been raised to respect the Constitution. The Communist Party, USA, certainly advocated a change from capitalism, with its private ownership of the means of production and a market economy driven by profit and greed, to a more equitable socialist economy. But we certainly respected the Constitution. It was a given: I would not cooperate with the Committee by answering their questions. But on what grounds would I refuse?

It seemed reasonable and appropriate that I would stand on First Amendment grounds and refuse to answer any questions related to ideas or assembly. I would be in good company. A few years earlier, Albert Einstein, responding in writing to a schoolteacher who faced dismissal because he had refused to testify before the Senate Internal Security Subcommittee, had written: "Frankly, I can see only the revolutionary way of non-cooperation in the sense of Gandhi's. Every intellectual who is called before one of the committees ought to refuse to testify, i.e., he must be prepared for jail and economic ruin, in short, for the sacrifice of his personal welfare in the interest of the cultural welfare of the country.

"This refusal to testify must be based on the assertion that it is shameful for a blameless citizen to submit to such an inquisition," the great scientist continued, "and that this kind of inquisition violates the spirit of the Constitution. When enough people are ready to take this grave step they will be successful. If not, then the intellectuals of this country deserve nothing better than the slavery which is intended for them" ("Einstein Counsels: 'Refuse to Testify,'" *New York Times*, June 12, 1953).

However, in 1957, the narrow options confronting witnesses subpoenaed by congressional committees after the Hollywood Ten's conviction seemed to have been expanded by the Supreme Court decision in the case of *Watkins v. United States*. John Thomas Watkins, an Illinois labor leader who had testified to HUAC that he had never been a member of the Communist Party but had cooperated with it, had answered Committee questions about people he knew to be Party members but had refused to answer questions about those who had left the Party. Tried and convicted of contempt, Watkins's case was reviewed by the Supreme Court, which overturned his conviction in a 6–1 decision written by Chief Justice Earl Warren. "When First Amendment rights are threatened, the delegation of power to the committee must be clearly revealed in its charter," Warren wrote. As Victor Rabinowitz later wrote in his memoir: "Here there was no such delegation of power. . . . While the power of the Congress to conduct investigations is inherent in the legislative process . . . broad as is this power of inquiry, it is not unlimited. There is no general authority to expose the private affairs of individuals without justification in terms of functions of the Congress. Investigations conducted solely for the personal aggrandizement of the investigators or to 'punish' those investigated are indefensible."

Jean and I were particularly struck by Justice Warren's query—"Who can define the meaning of the term 'un-American'?"—and thought that the *Watkins* decision might end the Committee. We reasoned that by affirming First Amendment rights as a basic principle of American democracy, and refusing to cooperate with HUAC, I could join an important struggle for civil liberties and help bring about that end.

I also had a more personal reason for refusing to answer the Committee's questions regarding Communist infiltration into the steel mills. In November 1956, Soviet forces had invaded Hungary to put down a popular revolt against the Communist government. I was very upset by the Soviet action and had said so at a small Communist Party meeting of a few steelworkers that was held in a comrade's home. That's when I had broken with the Party. The next morning, working the day shift, I had parked my car, and before I could open the door to get out, two men tapped on the window, identified themselves as FBI agents. Well, Ed, one of them asked, "Are you ready to talk to us now?" I, of course, responded that I had nothing to say to them, and walked away.

I remember this encounter as vividly as if it occurred yesterday—but how valid are my memories in my FBI file, which I obtained under the Freedom of Information Act in 1982, an unnamed FBI agent reported what I assume, because of the date, was a different conversation. "The subject was interviewed by Special Agent [redacted] on 1-29-57 as he was leaving his place of employment in the city of Gary, Indiana. The interview was conducted by [redacted] with [redacted] observing. The contact was made at about 4:25 p.m. and the interview lasted about fifteen minutes. . . . The Agent explained that the Bureau had known of his activities almost as soon as he had arrived in Gary, Indiana, and has kept up with them from day to day. He was told that in light of the Hungarian situation, it was felt he might have some change of heart and want to assist his government and the free world.

"Yellin said he was certain the government knew all about him and that he probably could give no additional information. He admitted that he had not always agreed with everything the CP [Communist Party] had done but nevertheless would not 'turn against his friends.' . . .

"Although Yellin appeared willing to listen to the Agent's plea, he did not appear friendly, did not show any inclination to continue the interview. He was not rude or curt in his statements, but showed no desire to cooperate."

I wonder why the report didn't mention that a few weeks before we left Gary for Colorado, I met with the district Party organizer, paid up my dues, and formally told him I was quitting.

After reading this memo from my FBI files, I did vaguely recall that although I was no longer bound by the CP's policy of never talking to an FBI agent, I felt confident that I would hold my own in a discussion with an FBI agent. Perhaps, then, I had spoken to them longer than I now recall.

In any event, if, as they claimed, the FBI knew all about me and the Gary Communist Party, they certainly would have shared their files with HUAC, and the Committee certainly would know that I had no information about "Communist subversion" and would not name names. Then why subpoena me? Clearly, the HUAC hearings were designed simply to expose CP members and create a climate of fear—and, just as clearly, I was not going to cooperate with them.

JEAN

When we had left Gary a half year before that sunny morning when Ed was served with the subpoena, it had become time—perhaps past time—to go. Our commitment to the Communist Party was gone, the Party itself was gone, and Ed had been burned—literally.

The children were in bed when Ed had appeared one night with his hands swathed in dressings, arms bandaged up to his elbows, accompanied by his foreman, who had driven him home. A furnace had "kicked," they explained, and although protective gear covered his head and neck, Ed had instinctively raised his arms to shield his head, burning his barely covered hands and arms. Following United States Steel procedures concerning accidents on the job, the foreman had taken him to the company clinic, then brought him home, promising to return at shift change in time to get him back to work. (Standard policy demanded that the foreman do whatever could be done to diminish insurance claims by keeping accidents off the books.)

Many years later, when we as a family talked about our remembrances of Gary and the case, two of our children recalled seeing their father's bandaged arms. You can see why that was the night we finally decided to leave Gary. This was not an easy decision. It was there that, as newlyweds, we had established our marriage, then built a home and a family. I feel that it was in Gary where I grew up and made friendships that ultimately were to last a lifetime. I vividly remember the day when I was at a bus stop downtown among a crowd of women, and suddenly, as in mining towns, the mill whistles screamed ACCIDENT. Every woman instantaneously stopped, turned toward the mill, and tried to reassure herself that her man was safe—every woman but me. At that moment, I realized that, despite having lived there for six years, birthing my three children and having a husband who worked in the mill, Gary was not truly home to me.

Nonetheless, we stayed on another two years. Like many other working-class families, we were living paycheck to paycheck and had zero savings. But the night Ed was burned, we decided to think about a different future. Ed enrolled in a college-level math course to see whether he could still do the work.

ED

I could! I enrolled in an integral calculus course at the Gary campus of Indiana University, studied hard, and did very well. So my ability to go back to school was not in question, but there was another force that made it a bit difficult to make the final decision. After working eight years in the open hearths at the largest steel mill in the country, I had really become a steel worker. I thought like one, and seniority was embedded in my psyche. Vacations, relocations, and layoffs were all based on seniority. It was hard for me to give up eight years of it. But I knew that it was time to go.

JEAN

That summer, we put our four-room clapboard house up for sale and began packing. When my sister Ann and her boys came to visit, we took tents and the five children and camped out at nearby Indiana Dunes State Park, while Ed continued to work shifts in the mill and did yet more packing.

A half century later, we still have the rocking chair I found while pregnant with Peter, and I can fondly remember the things I had collected for my babies—and furniture that we left behind. At the Salvation Army store I had bought a children's wardrobe chest, painted it light green, and decorated it with pictures of a train car on a track, with its two black wheels serving as handles. And I never will forget the wicker rocker for toddlers that I painted and then slipcovered in green denim. The furniture Ed had built was more substantial, and we planned to take that with us: a couch made from a door, a trundle bed for Peter and Lisa, a single bed that we acquired after Mike was born. Our grandchildren have since used them for years.

By summer's end, while Ann and I stayed with the children at the dunes, Ed packed the couch and children's beds, along with my mosaic-topped coffee table and our books, and we were on our way to Colorado. Why Ft. Collins? At the time, it seemed like a good idea for Ed to enroll at Colorado State University, where my older sister's husband taught. Paul and Mary were raising their four children on very little money, and we thought that they could teach us how to live economically. While CSU had a respectable engineering school, it was not highly competitive, and Ed understandably felt uncertain as to how well he could perform after eight years in the mill.

We moved into student quarters in Vet Village, emergency housing built during World War II by the army and later taken to campus to house the influx of veterans. Our Quonset—half of a circle built of corrugated steel divided into a living-dining-kitchen space, a tiny bathroom, and two small bedrooms—was on an unpaved road with a couple of trees in the dirt yard. It was, we thought, "good enough for who it's for." I recall sewing curtains with hems for rods top and bottom, because the walls curved in. We both became deeply involved in a co-op nursery school, as we had been in Gary, and our social life, such as it was, circled around my sister's family, our children, and their friends.

Peter was off in first grade, but three-year-old Lisa and two-year-old Mike were still in their pj's on that bright Colorado morning in January 1958 when the tall gentleman with the large Western hat knocked at our door and announced himself as a U.S. marshal.

CHAPTER TWO

Will Not/Cannot

ED

At the end of January, 1958, the *Gary Post-Tribune* announced that three days of hearings of the House Un-American Activities Committee were scheduled for February, and that eighteen subpoenas had been issued. Working from the standard Cold War script, in which the USSR was our diabolical enemy and "reds" were seen as traitors, for several days the paper publicized the event by printing the names, addresses, and places of employment of the men subpoenaed, by headlining a "Gary Counterspy" who would finger witnesses, and by announcing a "'Secret' Red Quiz Witness." They also published an editorial urging everyone to attend the sessions.

To our surprise, the paper also ran a full-page paid advertisement from the Calumet chapter of the Indiana Civil Liberties Union condemning HUAC and headlining the words of Chief Justice Earl Warren in the recent *Watkins v. United States* case: "Who can define the meaning of un-American?" Seeing this ad, we were heartened. It meant that the Civil Liberties Union people had gotten themselves together to challenge HUAC, and that the *Post-Tribune* had been willing to run their protest. Perhaps the Gary hearings might not simply repeat the McCarthy playbill.

As the Calumet Civil Liberties Union had noted, the Supreme Court, nine months earlier in *Watkins*, had asserted that congressional power is not unlimited, that the Court had been unable to ascertain the nature of the congressional inquiry under consideration, and that Congress has no authority to expose the private affairs of individuals. This decision had prompted the *New York Times* to comment (June 19, 1957) that "the Supreme Court has placed fundamental restrictions on a Congressional investigatory power that in recent years has been asserted as all but limitless." I had come to this HUAC hearing believing that by refusing to comply to their demands, I might contribute to the death knell of HUAC.

JEAN

I cannot recall leaving the children with sister Mary and traveling to Indiana. My indelible memory is of reaching the steps leading up to the Gary City Hall, getting separated from Ed and Vic, and knowing that there was no way that I could get up those crowded stairs. Then I felt a firm grip steering my elbow. A friend and fellow nursery-school parent was somehow pushing me up the steps, saying, "Mrs. Yellin has no comment to make."

The city council chamber was ugly, large, dark, and packed. People were sitting awkwardly on folding chairs with jackets, scarves, and coats draped over the backs. The first rows were roped off for the high school civics students, and the next were crammed with men wearing their Veterans of Foreign Wars and American Legion caps. The smell of wet wool and galoshes was strong. At the front were two large tables, one for the HUAC congressmen and their staff. The other was surrounded by empty chairs awaiting witnesses and their lawyers. In an interview, Victor Rabinowitz, Ed's attorney, later recalled, "I felt it was enemy territory that I was walking into, that it was very hostile. Really! [Frank] Tavenner, the lawyer for the Committee, and its members, were putting on a road show in which they would go from place to place. The Committee was riding high. It was at the height of its power."

More than a half century later, recalling those HUAC hearings and reading through the transcript, I don't know whether to laugh or cry. I do both. The situation was certainly not funny! Eleven steelworkers had been subpoenaed by two members of the 85th Congress in an investigation of "Communist Infiltration and Propaganda Activities in Basic Industry." After the formal opening, the "secret witness" promised by the *Post-Tribune* appeared. He was John Lautner, a professional witness who for years had been testifying before HUAC in the red hunt. (Five years earlier Lautner had already produced "several thousand pages of testimony" against communism, according to Herbert L. Packer's 1962 book from Stanford University Press, *Ex-Communist Witnesses: Four Studies in Fact Finding—A Challenging Examination of the Testimony of Whittaker Chambers, Elizabeth Bentley, Louis Budenz, and John Lautner*).

In Gary, Lautner swore that after a long career as a Communist "functionary," he had been expelled from the Party in 1950 after being "subjected to indignities and tortures" in a Cleveland basement by three Communist leaders. Instructed by Communism's "international leadership" to "get rid of me fast," Party leaders had questioned him about his connections with the FBI and CIA while threatening him with butcher knives, rubber hoses, and guns.

Having theatrically described a violent international Communist conspiracy, Lautner turned to the subject of the day, the efforts of the American Communist Party to colonize basic industries. This was a topic with which the congressmen were very familiar: Four years earlier, HUAC had published a booklet, "Colonization of America's Basic Industries by the Communist Party of the U.S.A." Lautner detailed a Party policy of persuading bright young college men "that a so-called bourgeois education and diploma have no future" and that a better future lay in becoming "the leaders of large segments of workers in basic industries." After reciting a tale that would fill sixteen pages of fine print, he sat down to the congressmen's effusive praise.

Then Ed was called. After he gave his name and current address, Vic interrupted the proceedings. Aware that House rules specified that committees must respond to witnesses' requests for an executive session (without the presence of the public and the press), Vic noted that he had sent telegrams to HUAC requesting such for his client but had received no response. When he now

requested that the record show that he had made this application, he was cut off by Rep. Francis Walter, who announced, "we
will decide whether it will be made a part of the record when the
executive session is held. Go ahead." Vic tried again to ensure
that the transcripts would include his request, but was stopped
cold by the chairman: "You know the privileges given you by this
committee. You have appeared before it often enough. You know
as well as anybody."

I was sitting near the windows a few rows back, straining to hear
and struggling to understand what was happening in the front of
the room. I had no idea that this exchange over the request for an
executive session would, five years later, keep Ed out of jail.

Trying to hear what Ed was saying, I realized that instead of
stating where he had lived before September 1957, he was asserting
that he wanted "to state my grounds as to what my position will be
on answering questions."

Sitting in that dismal room, I understood that by directing Ed to
answer their questions, HUAC was creating a record to enable them
to cite him for contempt of Congress and send him to jail, and that
Ed was basing his refusals to answer not on the self-incrimination
section of the Fifth Amendment, but on the freedom of speech and
association guaranteed by the First Amendment. Ed was challenging HUAC's right to question him—their right to exist.

ED

It was like a Hollywood movie. Vic had held me by the elbow and
steered Jean and me up the hundreds, no, thousands of steps leading to the city council chambers, while pushing aside what seemed
like an army of reporters shouting questions that mixed with
the sounds of stamping feet and resonated in the large hallway. I
hardly noticed that we had separated from Jean as Vic and I were
directed to a side door and seated at a table facing the growing
crowd of schoolchildren in the front rows, followed by older men,
many wearing their American Legion and VFW caps.

I started rehearsing in my head the recommendations that Vic had discussed with me the night before: Do not come with what appears to be a long prepared statement that you expect to read. The chair will not allow it. Instead, use scraps of paper on which you have written your ideas for possible responses to the obvious questions. Try not to read your notes, but use them as reminders of responses to the expected questions.

A few minutes after 10 a.m., the Committee members and staff walked in and sat at a table facing Vic and me and a few others whom I did not recognize. The chairman, Rep. Francis E. Walter (D-PA), introduced himself and the other member, Rep. Gordon H. Scherer (R-OH), and the two staff members, Frank S. Tavenner Jr., counsel, and Raymond T. Collins, investigator. Walters then read for the record a series of statements, laws, relevant background information, purposes of the hearing, and so forth. The first witness was John Lautner, a "friendly witness" who set the stage for the hearing. I was next.

Tavenner asked all the questions, while Walters often engaged me in brief discussions and, in his role as chair, directed me to answer several questions (a witness could only be cited for contempt if he was directed by the chair to answer and refused). Scherer occasionally asked Walter to direct me to answer, or interjected a remark to emphasize a point.

Very early in my testimony, Scherer got ahead of himself in his haste to get to the matter of "conspiracy." When Tavenner asked, "Mr. Yellin, where did you reside prior to September 1957?," I took the opportunity to state what my position will be on answering the Committee's questions, as follows:

"Mr. Walter, I do not feel that this is the place for myself, as an individual and as a citizen, to discuss my beliefs, my associations, or whatever expressions of opinions I have ever made. I feel that ideas in the democratic process should be settled, should reach some kind of an understanding, in the marketplace of ideas and not at a Congressional investigation. I believe the entire democratic process revolves around settling things in a free and open market, and this is not the place for it. This is a hearing. It is not an expression of public opinion."

Scherer then interjected: "We are not asking you about your

ideas or opinions. We are asking you about your activities within the conspiracy."

"We are asking his address," Chairman Walter noted, scolding Scherer for jumping to conspiracy.

This was followed by some back and forth between myself and Walter and between Vic and Walter concerning the recent *Watkins* and *Sweeny* cases and the *Lloyd Barenblatt* case, all concerning HUAC and the First Amendment. After I commented on the *Watkins* case, perhaps not entirely accurately, Walter responded that he would "straighten me out" on the case. Then Vic interrupted:

"As a lawyer, Mr. Chairman, I would like the opportunity to straighten you out. But I guess this is not the chance."

"Your kind of lawyer could not straighten me out on anything," Walter replied. "Go ahead, please."

The transcript continues:

MR. YELLIN: *May I continue, Mr. Congressman? I am not a lawyer.*

MR. TAVENNER: *Let me interrupt you for a minute. You constantly referred to "this line of questioning." The only question I have asked you is where did you live prior to September 1957. . . . Certainly one question cannot be construed as a line of questioning. You have been asked only one question.*

MR. YELLIN: *May I continue?*

THE CHAIRMAN: *Why don't you answer the question? Where did you live?*
That is all we want to know.

MR. YELLIN: *I heard the previous witness. I read proceedings of this committee in past cases. I read the newspapers concerning the history of this committee. If I say this line of questioning, I should say this particular question. It is pretty obvious where this question will lead from what has gone before. So it is no sense in pinning it down and waiting to later. It is going to lead to a certain point. There is no question about that.*

In retrospect, I can't believe that I was that tongue-tied at thirty! In 1958 I had been a student, sailor, steelworker, and student again. I had no experience in addressing an audience and certainly not in being questioned by a congressional committee. Today, after a thirty-five-year career as a scientist and professor, and after having lectured to students and to my peers in scientific meetings, I am much more poised at presenting ideas and at ease when being questioned, sometimes forcibly, by my peers. Of course, being questioned by a congressional committee, and one that was hostile to my ideas, is very different from being questioned by colleagues. Presenting my research to colleagues who may push me hard to justify my conclusions is a pleasure because I have faith in my data and its interpretation.

Back to the hearing: The grounds on which I objected to the proceedings were that the First Amendment to the Constitution specifically says that Congress shall make no law abridging the freedom of speech; therefore, Congress cannot investigate in that area because they cannot legislate in that area. Furthermore, I had committed no unlawful acts; therefore, any questioning could only be investigating my conscience, my personal beliefs, my opinions, expressions, and associations.

Furthermore, I said, the enabling resolution by which Congress had established HUAC was very vague, and therefore opened the possibility that I would not be accorded my rights under due process of law, because the courts would not be able to properly judge the intent of this committee. The courts had already ruled, however, that the only questions this committee could ask me as an individual were questions pertinent to legislation. Therefore, I concluded, "I don't feel that this question is pertinent to any legislation the committee might be investigating and furthermore, as I said before, the committee cannot even investigate legislation pertaining to the First Amendment. Therefore, I will have to respectfully submit that I cannot answer" the question about where I had resided.

For me, "cannot answer" displayed my commitment more deeply than "will not answer." Chairman Walter picked up on that: "You said, 'I cannot.' Of course you are not under any prohibition. You could answer it. You mean, 'I will not'."

I replied, "I cannot under my own moral conscience."

"Then you do not answer the question for these reasons, is that it?"

"Yes, sir."

"All right," Walter said.

I like the subtlety of what I said because at thirty I was more likely to respond from the gut than from the cerebellum. As a child and a teenager, I had judged my friends on their ability on the soft-ball field or the handball court, not on their intellectual prowess. When I told my mother that I had a new friend, she would always ask (in Yiddish) "*Iz er a kluger?*," that is, "Is he clever?," and I invariably said something like "Who cares, he's great on the ballfield!"

Scherer then intervened: "Now, Mr. Chairman, so that the record is clear, I ask that you direct the witness to answer the question."

Walter directed me to answer the question: "Where did you live prior to September 1957?"

I refused again.

Tavenner asked: "You do not rely, in your refusal to answer, upon the self-incriminating clause of the Fifth Amendment. Is that correct?"

The transcript continues:

MR. YELLIN. *That is correct. I am relying on my First Amendment rights.*

MR. TAVENNER. *You were present when the opening statement was made by the chairman of this committee, were you not?*

MR. YELLIN. *Yes sir; I was present at that time.*

MR. TAVENNER. *This is a hearing which involves a subject described by the chairman, and it relates to Communist Party activities within the area of Gary. As far as pertinency of the question is concerned, as to which you seem to express some doubt, it would be impossible for us to learn anything from you regarding Communist Party activities in this area without ascertaining whether or not you were here for a period of time. Now, having explained that and given you that reason as a basis for the committee's asking you that question, I would like ask the chair to again direct the witness to answer.*

THE CHAIRMAN. *You are directed to answer.*

Another "I cannot" . . . "You mean do not" exchange followed before the questioning turned to my formal educational training.

JEAN

Two of Ed's university transcripts were put into evidence, with special attention paid to the dates of his attendance and his "grade of A in many subjects." Also put into evidence was his 1949 job application at U.S. Steel, on which he had recorded no education beyond high school, claiming that he had worked at various jobs during the years his college records showed him in attendance. Ed was directed by the chair to answer a question pertaining to Communist colonization of the steelworkers' union in Gary; Ed refused to answer. Next there were questions aimed at establishing Ed's membership in the Communist Party before and during his time in Gary. He again refused to answer, citing his previously stated reasons and, under questioning by Scherer, reiterating that his refusal was not based on his Fifth Amendment rights. The final question that Ed was directed to answer and refused again "on the grounds already stated" was, "Are you a member of the Communist Party now?"

Another question that Ed refused to answer despite being directed by the chair to answer had interesting consequences. Tavenner asked, "Will you tell the committee what stand the Communist Party took in Gary in any of its units with regards to the acts of the Soviet Union in Hungary in 1956?"

ED

At a small Communist Party meeting held in a comrade's home early in November 1956, I had vigorously objected to the Soviet invasion of Hungary, which put down a popular uprising against Soviet domination. The Hungarian people, I explained, had a right to self-determination. My position was counter to that of the Party, which had been slavishly backing the position of the Soviet Union regarding its dominance of the Warsaw Pact countries.

The next day, as I arrived at the steel mill parking lot, before I could even open the car door, two well-dressed men tapped on the window. I rolled it down a bit, and one of the men asked, "Well, Ed, are you ready to talk to us now?" I replied "no" and proceeded to head toward the mill gate, with no further words said.

I was more than curious as to how the FBI knew what had gone on at the meeting. I couldn't believe that any of the comrades had informed, so I assumed that the house was bugged.

Soon after the HUAC hearing in Gary, I was cited for contempt of Congress by the full committee and by the House of Representatives for my failure to answer five questions. A few months later, an indictment was handed down by a grand jury in Hammond, Indiana, citing my refusal to answer four of those five questions. The one about the Soviet invasion of Hungary was excluded. Why so?

My FBI files much later revealed, not unexpectedly, that I was a "person of interest" who had to be observed and occasionally contacted by an FBI agent. Count five may have been dropped from my charges because it would have been clear that the FBI had given the information to HUAC, and for some reason they did not want that to become public. It is also probable that if I went to trial the FBI almost certainly did not want to be questioned on how they knew what went on at that Party meeting. Incidentally, even though the FBI knew I was no longer a member of the CP, I remained a "person of interest" for many years because of my refusal to cooperate with HUAC.

JEAN

After drinking nearly an entire pitcher of water and smoking a dozen cigarettes, Ed was finally dismissed, and the hearings broke for lunch.

Fleeing the building, we hurriedly picked up the early edition of the *Post-Tribune* and noted the banner headline: "Ex-Gary Man 'Mum' at Quiz/Pleads 1st Amendment to Salons/Yellin Testimony Stirs Clashes at Steel Mill Red Inquiry." We skipped lunch and caught the next South Shore commuter train back to Chicago and the Illinois Central on to Denver, to our children, to Ed's eighteen credits of classes, and to our lives. As a result, we missed hearing the testimony of the four steelworkers and the local stool pigeon that afternoon, as well as the proceedings of the second day, when ten more men were questioned by the Committee.

CHAPTER THREE

Surprised and Shocked

ED

Retrieving the children from their abrupt stay with their cousins at Jean's sister Mary's house, we went home to our Quonset, and I became immersed in my classes again. I was carrying a full course load: engineering electronics, mechanical engineering lab, mechanical design and studies in mechanical design, something called industrial organization, and an honors colloquium.

On March 4, after our family joyously celebrated Lisa's fourth birthday, I wrote a long letter to Professor J. Taylor Strate, my department head, expressing heartfelt gratitude for being nominated for a Westinghouse Scholarship, the highest honor the department could grant an undergraduate. I outlined my academic past, my current situation, and my hopes for the future: "Basically, I enjoy the challenge of problem solving. I believe I could be happy studying and working with my hands and my head, and I gain great satisfaction from the finished products resulting from my labor." Turning to the issue at hand, I continued, "I am very aware of the enormous value of the individual recognition and prestige afforded the recipient of a Westinghouse Scholarship. Of equal, if not more value to me, however, would be the financial aid."

JEAN

Ed was becoming accustomed to academic stress. He no longer needed to make flash cards of various equations with which I would drill him. I was glad to relinquish my tutorial role.

But what he wrote in his letter to Professor Strate was surely true. For five people living on a budget of $3,040 for the academic year, that $500 Westinghouse Scholarship was big money. We whooped with delight when Ed received the formal letter announcing it. But our joy was quickly dispelled.

Two weeks later, on April 17, we felt HUAC's long reach. A reporter from the *Denver Post* phoned and read a wire service release announcing Ed's citation on four counts for contempt of Congress. Ed responded that he was "surprised and shocked," and said he would have a statement for them in the afternoon. The *Post* ran a brief item reporting the contempt citation: "The House Un-American Activities Committee recommended Wednesday a contempt citation against six former witnesses. . . . Among the six was Edward Yellin, a former Gary steel worker. Yellin told the *Denver Post* Thursday morning the committee action 'comes as a complete surprise to me.' He said he will make no statement on the recommended citation or the circumstances of the Gary hearing '"until I've had a chance to think this thing over.'"

ED

"Surprised and shocked" was to become my standard rejoinder to reporters over the next years as honors and awards given to me were then revoked. The first time, however, was all shook up. The morning of the call, I wrote to a good friend: "I don't mind facing the committee, because you do it once, know where you stand, and you're finished—at least for a while—but the thought of the local paper getting the news, and me having to explain to I don't know how many people, how many times, is not something to look forward to."

Our local paper was mum on the subject, however, and I quickly settled down, confident that the Supreme Court would be willing to hear my case and would rule in my favor. "But for the time being," I wrote to my friend, "it isn't likely that the Justice Department will roll full speed ahead against the hundred or more citations that haven't yet been acted on. At any rate, it would be nice to get through one academic quarter without a major event to distract me."

JEAN

That small *Post* piece was all State Farm Insurance needed to cancel our auto policy. Fort Collins had no public transportation; how could we manage without a car? Our attempts to find a local insurance broker were utterly fruitless until we reached a friend in Gary who was working part-time as an insurance salesman, and he convinced his boss to cover us. I felt tremendous relief: I would be able to get to the grocery store. (We later learned from our friend that State Farm had not cancelled for political reasons, but because Ed's name had appeared in a news story, which might influence a juror if Ed, or even I, were to be involved in a liability issue.)

Immediately after the call from the *Post* reporter, Ed and I realized that it was time to have a discussion with Professor Strate, to prepare him for the story that might eventually be reported by the local newspaper. Ed called and asked to meet with Strate to "discuss an important issue." They met at Strate's home, not far from campus.

ED

I'll never forget that meeting! We sat in his living room, and I looked out his picture window and watched the sun set over the Rocky Mountains as he tried in vain to understand what was happening to his favorite student.

His first reaction: I'm entitled to my beliefs, and he respects any man who defends his ideas, but I had made an error in judgment. Over and over again he asked, "If you are no longer a member of the Communist Party, why not go to the FBI and clear your name?"—and over and over again I tried to explain that HUAC had violated my constitutional rights and that there shouldn't be a need to "clear my name."

Eventually he said that he didn't want to ask any more questions because the less he knew, the less he would be obliged to tell any prospective employer or the FBI. Strate was shocked by my news, and immediately thought the FBI might question him because he had gotten me the Westinghouse, and because Colorado State University was a land-grant school with purse strings controlled by a state legislature that loved to find an excuse for a stink.

JEAN

Another event triggered by that *Post* article involved a young Israeli couple. Mika was studying at Colorado State because of its world-class reputation in hydraulics and water conservation. He and his wife, Shoshi, stopped by often to socialize with us and play with our children. This day, they appeared in the morning and stayed and stayed and stayed. As the day wore on, they explained that they had read about American McCarthyism, and had decided to come to protect us from the mob.

Fortunately, there were no mobs in Fort Collins, and in the shadow of the mountains we could almost forget about HUAC—almost.

Spring was graduation season, and with it came the annual awards dinner, which included the announcement of Ed's Westinghouse Scholarship. That afternoon, Ed returned to our Quonset in amazement. He knew that his department chair had discussed Ed's HUAC experience with the dean of the engineering college, and he thought it likely that all the administrative officers would also know. Ed came home to tell me that the dean of students had called him into his office to inform him that the university would not be giving him the award that night because they feared that it

might jeopardize their relationship with Westinghouse. The dean acted as though the revocation was a one-time action, and without the slightest recognition of the absurdity of what he was about to say, he assured Ed that he could apply again.

Undeterred, we marched on. In addition to studying, keeping house, and tending the children, we spent Ed's senior year exploring which universities might award financial support for a student of mechanical engineering seeking a PhD—and what kind of political climate we might find at them.

We knew that as early as 1947, responding to government claims of Communist subversion, the American Association of University Professors had boldly declared that affiliation with the Communist Party "in and of itself should not be regarded as a justifiable reason for exclusion from the academic profession." But the association, writes Ellen Schrecker in her 1986 study, *No Ivory Tower: McCarthyism and the Universities* (Oxford University Press), never enforced its report. Schrecker notes that in 1949, following the findings of the Washington State Un-American Activities Committee, the University of Washington fired three tenured professors, and by 1953, in the face of HUAC's upcoming series of hearings on higher education, the Association of American Universities, consisting of the presidents of thirty-seven institutions, issued a statement identifying world communism as the central threat to academic freedom, and announcing that "present membership in the Communist Party . . . extinguishes the right to a university position."

The next year, Chandler Davis, a young mathematician on the faculty of the University of Michigan, stood on the First Amendment to refuse to answer HUAC's questions while challenging the legitimacy of the entire inquiry. Ultimately, he and two of his colleagues were fired, and Davis went to jail for contempt of Congress.

We needed to find the right place to continue Ed's studies and raise our children. Ed was offered graduate assistantships at Berkeley, Purdue, and Michigan. He turned down a full-time IBM fellowship at Cornell without knowing of the HUAC-inspired travails of Phillip Morrison and Marcus Singer at that university. Instead—unaware of the treatment of musicologist Norman Cazden, who four years earlier, instead of being promoted, had been dismissed at the University of Illinois after the president showed him an anonymous document claiming he was a Communist—Ed accepted a fellowship at the University of Illinois' new Ford Foundation program in Urbana.

ED

Before accepting the offer, I had to decide whether I should inform the university of my contempt of Congress citation. If I revealed my background, it could easily lead to a revocation of the offer, but if I held back and the university later discovered my situation, I could be accused of not being forthcoming. I was definitely between a rock and a hard place. Jean and I thought long and hard before making a decision. We reasoned that because I had not yet been convicted of a crime, and also because I had not been interviewed before I was offered the fellowship, we decided to "let sleeping dogs lie," and I did not mention my appearance before HUAC. My fellowship carried a first-year grant of $3,000, a second-year grant of $2,600, and a $3,000-per-year loan provision, with the loans forgiven at the rate of $600 for each year of teaching.

JEAN

On June 5, 1959, Colorado State University awarded Ed his bachelor's degree with highest honors. The children and I thought him extremely handsome in his robes. We watched with his mother who, upon learning of his subpoena to the HUAC hearings in Gary, had offered him support by writing, "Don't be nervous. Be brave, like I used to be in my young years." So very proud of her son, she had flown from the Bronx to revel in the pleasure of watching Ed receive his diploma. After her fleeting visit—during which we chanted, "Not to worry, not to worry"—we drove her to the Denver airport, and within days packed up and were on our way to Urbana.

Five people camping in an 8'x8' tent made us all ripe. Although it was against our principles (really, against our budget), by the time we reached St. Louis, we decided to spring for a motel with showers. With the kids washed, fed, and settled down, Ed and I waited for them to doze off, then climbed over their sleeping bags and headed for the motel lobby. On the newspaper rack, the front page of the *St. Louis Post-Dispatch* screamed out that the Supreme Court had decided 5–4 to affirm the conviction in the *Barenblatt* case. Lloyd Barenblatt would go to jail for relying on the First Amendment.

We did not understand the difference between this decision and the Court's decision two years before in *Watkins*—the case on which Ed had relied in refusing to cooperate with HUAC. As Victor Rabinowitz, our attorney, would later write in his 1996 memoir, *Unrepentant Leftist* (University of Illinois Press), "it is extremely difficult . . . to justify the difference of results in the two cases. Like most Supreme Court cases, and in fact like most cases of any kind, there are extralegal political and philosophical considerations that motivate judges."

What we did understand was that our lives were about to change. Would Ed be the next to go to prison? If so, when?

We couldn't go back to Fort Collins: Ed had his diploma, and we had given up our Quonset. There seemed no better path than continuing on to Illinois. When we anxiously phoned Victor in New York from the motel lobby payphone, he tried to reassure us that it was extremely unlikely that a federal grand jury would be called in Indiana during the summer. We should continue coming east, he said, settle in Urbana, and have Ed enroll at the university, as planned.

So we did. Because the university had no openings in student family housing, we rented a small frame house on a leafy street and, recalling the concerns of Mika and Shoshana, went to the pound and adopted a large Doberman Pinscher to protect us. (Already named Blitz, we changed his moniker to the more peaceful "Shalom," but when our daughter Lisa couldn't remember it, we compromised with Blintz—which both the child and the dog could handle.)

After the tiny Quonset hut, it felt lovely to be in the little house with its basement and backyard. The trees and the grass were pleasant, and the elementary school the children would attend was only two blocks away. Our new neighbors, small businessmen, low-level executives, and housewives, were unconnected to the university and uninvolved with campus life. After Colorado, it all felt very familiar, very Midwestern: there was no post-football game shooting at campus streetlights; no students in wide-brimmed hats calling me "Ma'am." It felt normal.

Summer classes were well under way when, on July 15, the *Gary Post-Tribune* was headlined "Smash Dope Peddlers' Ring Here; Arrest 25." In "a sweeping series of overnight arrests," the article said, ten agents of the Chicago office of the Federal Bureau of Narcotics had joined about fifteen local detectives in seizing $100,000 worth of drugs and arresting twenty-five men and women. With the local prison suddenly overwhelmed, a federal grand jury was quickly convened. It promptly indicted the twenty-five on drug charges—and also brought indictments against four "unfriendly" HUAC witnesses on charges of contempt of Congress: Ed, Al Samter, Vic Malis, and Bob Lehrer.

ED

Alarmed when they learned of my indictment, family and friends back in Goldens Bridge announced a support meeting with a 25¢ admission, refreshments, and a talk by Jean's sister, Ann, titled "The Supreme Court, Civil Liberties, and You." This show of support touched me, recalling warm memories of Goldens Bridge and the Coops. To our supporters, I reviewed the situation: "It means a very great deal to know there are people—albeit in Goldens Bridge, a thousand miles away—who are with us, and willing to help. The case will probably be in the courts for years, and is terribly wearing, emotionally and financially Now, when the axe has fallen, the value and meaning of your support becomes really clear."

I lived a complicated existence that summer. In addition to a math class (Complex Variables and Applications), I found a part-time laboratory job, which, like all state employment, required me to sign the Broyles Bill oath declaring that I was not a Communist. At that time I was not, but I signed reluctantly, distressed at complying with the repressive oath. In August, I joined the other Ford interns for a five-day orientation.

Soon after, I also became acquainted with the criminal justice system. The four of us who had been indicted were ordered by the circuit court in Hammond, Indiana, to appear for arraignment. Fingerprinted and photographed, all of us pleaded not guilty. My bail was set at $1,000, but I was released on my own recognizance and fortunately did not have to post bail. Borrowing $1,000 at 11 percent interest would have taken too large a chunk out of our meager finances.

JEAN

The children and I went to Indiana with Ed, but we did not attend the arraignment. It was that weekend that Ed and I learned that on the fateful Monday afternoon when we had fled the Gary hearings to get back to Fort Collins and our children, three men had followed Ed's lead, refusing to testify and citing the First Amendment, while a fourth, alone among the witnesses, had also claimed the self-incrimination protection of the Fifth Amendment. The afternoon HUAC session had ended with the testimony of the local stool pigeon, Joe LaFleur, who had recited name after name of people he claimed were Party members. When finished, he received an accolade from Rep. Walter, emphasizing the contribution of HUAC to the Cold War: "Your contribution may be as great as a division in the Army."

We also learned that the Calumet area American Civil Liberties Union had issued a public letter denouncing the Gary hearings and urging the Indiana congressional delegation to "take early leadership for revocation of the mandate of the House Committee on Un-American Activities." Additionally, they had sent letters to the management of U.S. Steel, Inland Steel, and Youngstown Sheet and Tube, asking that they not fire any employees who "merely had claimed Constitutional privileges against testifying," and had sent a delegation to the steelworkers union for the same purpose. In a *Post-Tribune* interview (February 20, 1958), the ACLU chapter president, Mario Tomsich, had reiterated the demand that Congress cut the appropriation of HUAC, pointing out that "for the subpoenaed men, their wives and children, the stigma of having been called by HUAC remains," as well as "possible loss of jobs, union position and status in community organizations."

While the newspaper coverage had been quite full, we were surprised to learn that the hearings had sparked only one exchange of letters to the editor of the *Post-Tribune*. Frances Malis, whose husband had testified, wrote that, "at the hearing, she sat in a daze, waiting for the 'honorable' witness to name the crimes against my husband." One reader wrote in, attacking her letter. That was it: there was no further public discussion of the hearings.

ED

Years later, attempting to learn more about the hearings' aftermath, we talked to the other "unfriendly" HUAC witnesses charged with contempt of Congress.

The happiest story we heard was from Al Samter, an assistant grievance committeeman in the union, who had been indicted with me. He reported that a few workers had made nasty remarks in the wash house, but that his fellow assistant grievance committeemen supported him. Nonetheless, they asked him to resign because a union election was imminent, and he did quit after making a formal statement that he was resigning only because he did not want to confuse that election with any other issues. Al had moved into a new subdivision with his wife and two young children, where everyone was having problems with the builder. When they had organized to demand restitution, Al had been chosen as their secretary, but after the HUAC hearings, they called a secret meeting to throw him out. Discovering this, Al went to the meeting and explained his position: "HUAC had no more right to deny me my First Amendment rights than the steel company has to deny me my rights under our contract. The organizers of the meeting had backed off."

Although Vic Malis and his four brothers had been featured in the press after testifying on the second day of the hearings, they had not met together to discuss their testimony, before or after. Each had handled the situation in his own way. Chris Malis reported that some of his fellow steelworkers got up a petition to throw him out, but it never went to the union or anywhere else.

When Bob Lehrer was indicted, he was a student in the graduate school of education at the University of Chicago. He had decided to base his refusal to testify on the First Amendment because he thought it was the right thing to do; when his lawyer had pointed out that he might go to jail, Lehrer had responded, "Okay. Someone has to make the argument against HUAC." Speaking with university colleagues about the indictment, he had found them sympathetic. His indictment did not disturb his schoolwork, but he was sure that it would affect where he could apply for a teaching job—only at schools that did not include a noncommunist disclaimer in their application.

The saddest story we heard involved the only witness, Jack Kretheotes, who had claimed the protection of the Fifth Amendment, although he had also cited the First Amendment. He was, of course, not in danger of indictment. As Al recalled, however, Jack "did not deal with this like the rest of us. He did not take a forth-right position, but was hedging his bets." In the mill, his fellow workers gave him a hard time. The principal of his children's school wanted them thrown out. His marriage fell apart. Frances Malis recalled that when, in an effort to show support, she had invited them to share a family outing, his wife had declined, saying she didn't want to be associated with well-known Reds.

I realized that my confidence and ability to fight back were based, in large measure, on the fact that my Goldens Bridge friends and several others had responded to us so warmly and generously. The other Gary indictees had no comparable support, and their morale had suffered for it. The contrast was startling to us.

JEAN

By September, with Ed immersed in his coursework, I had some-how gotten my credentials in order and found a job as a part-time teacher of homebound children. (I, too, signed the Broyles oath.) When the school year opened, Michael started nursery school and I started work. Our December 1959 family newsletter included reports from all of us: Peter, in third grade, wrote that he planned to become a college football player before going pro, then a base-ball player; Lisa was worrying about a loose tooth and reported that she enjoyed being dressed at Halloween as Little Red Riding Hood; Mike stated that he liked to pet Blintz. Clearly, normalcy was reigning on Foley Street.

When our doorbell rang one afternoon, Ed and I found our-selves face to face with a woman and very tall man who greeted us in a strong Brooklyn accent: "We hear that you folks are in trou-ble." Recently arrived in Urbana, Louise and Aaron Bindman had heard from Chicago friends about Ed's HUAC experience and had come to help. And help they did: with their children Tina and Andy providing playmates for Lisa and Mike (Peter was odd man out), they offered us comradeship—and a home where we could leave the kids when Ed and I drove back up to Hammond to hear our lawyers' arguments urging dismissal of Ed's indictment.

No luck. The judge set Ed's trial date for March. We soon learned that the psychology professor Lloyd Barenblatt had begun serving six months in federal prison for relying on the First Amendment when refusing to testify to HUAC about his political beliefs.

Ed added his name to a newly formed "Committee of First Amendment Defendants" and read with interest the group's analysis (from a November 4, 1959 press conference): "The *Barenblatt* decision has cleared the way for the processing of a number of other 'First Amendment Cases' which have been held up in the courts, some as long as four years, pending a final ruling in this definitive case. More than thirty defendants in various parts of the country are involved in these 'contempt' cases . . . [resulting] from the refusal of witnesses to answer any or all questions put to them by HUAC or the Senate Internal Security Subcommittee." By year's end, a Chicago group organizing around the First Amendment invited Ed to become involved. Ed and I drove to Chicago to attend a meeting, but Ed was critical of the nearly complete absence of young people. "We are," he wrote to the committee, "faced with a situation where more people are going to jail than at the height of McCarthyism, and yet the public thinks that McCarthyism is dead. Neither the [HUAC] hearings nor the indictments are in the headlines. Surely the 'old timers' have to be moved into action, but we will hardly make a dent if we cannot reach and convince more people."

The point was well taken: In all of the years that Senator Joseph McCarthy had spent attacking our freedoms, he had not sent a single person to prison. Now, in 1959, for the first time since the Hollywood Ten were jailed by HUAC in 1947, and with McCarthy discredited and three years dead, people were being locked up for their thoughts, or for their refusal to become informers about the thoughts of others. This marked the beginning of a new offensive on civil liberties, at a time when most people thought the witch hunt was over.

By the new year, not only Lloyd Barenblatt but also Willard Uphaus, Paul Rosenkrantz, and H. Chandler Davis, all four victims of McCarthyism, were behind bars. Would Ed be next?

CHAPTER FOUR

Lacking Contrition

JEAN

Ed was tried for contempt of Congress in the federal district court in Hammond, Indiana, on Tuesday, March 8, 1960. Now thirty-three years old, he was found guilty and sentenced on Thursday, March 10. While we were both at his trial, neither of us, strangely, can recall much about it. We were stunned. We've had to go through old correspondence and newspaper clippings to remind ourselves what happened during those three days. What we both recall is our deep anxiety about the process and the outcome.

ED

One thing we do vividly remember is dining with our lawyer, Vic Rabinowitz, at Chicago's premier hotel, the Palmer House, the night before the trial. Being rubes, we were more impressed with the service and décor—including an ice sculpture—than with the food. The highlight of the dinner was when the maître d', noticing me taking out a cigarette, raced across the floor "faster than a speeding bullet" and flipped open his lighter. Naively, I thought, not bad for a guy who in 1960 saw himself as a street kid from "da Bronx," a former Gary steelworker, now a graduate student fighting for his right to be silent.

Preparing for the trial, Vic was acutely aware that the Supreme Court ruling in the *Barenblatt* case had changed everything. The Court had functionally overruled their *Watkins* decision, on which my refusal to testify was based. Because of this change, instead of rearguing the classic First Amendment position asserting the primacy of freedom of speech and association—the argument that had repeatedly lost in court—both Vic and sister Ann advised that it would be best to base our argument on the new decision in *Barenblatt*: "Where First Amendment rights are asserted to bar governmental interrogation, resolution of the issue always involves a balancing by the courts of the competing private and public interests at stake in the particular circumstances shown."

I had read the *Barenblatt* decision when it was announced in June, and had felt extremely disappointed that the Court was not interpreting First Amendment rights as primary. Nevertheless, since the justices now evidently thought it important to "balance" an individual's right to privacy with the public's demand for "security," we were preparing to argue that my need to maintain the privacy of my ideas, as well as the need of the public in a democracy to hear all kinds of ideas, outbalanced HUAC's need to elicit my testimony.

We now had to decide on whether to have a judge or a "jury of our peers" decide my case. We knew back then what, according to Robert Lichtman's 2012 book, *The Supreme Court and McCarthy-Era Repression* (University of Illinois Press), a 1954 study by the Fund for the Republic, a unit of the Ford Foundation, had found, in examining "attitudes on communism, conformity, and civil liberties," that "public opinion would support virtually any sanction imposed on Communists," with 89 percent believing that a Communist should be fired from a college teaching job, 68 percent that he should be fired from clerking in a store, 77 percent that he should be stripped of citizenship, and 51 percent that he should be jailed. And we also remembered, oh so clearly, being spat on by people whom we had approached on the streets of Gary to sign the 1950 Stockholm Peace Appeal, an international petition, illustrated by Pablo Picasso's peace dove, to outlaw nuclear weapons. More than one petitioner had even been arrested or threatened by the police.

In this environment, I thought I didn't have much choice: I opted for a bench trial—no jury. Given the Cold War political climate, I thought a jury would probably be more hostile than a judge—particularly a judge like Luther M. Swygert who, perhaps because he was a Roosevelt appointee, was thought to be a somewhat liberal man.

JEAN

On the day of Ed's trial in March 1960, the *Gary Post-Tribune* reported a mob of spectators overflowing the hall, but the morning's early courtroom events included naturalization ceremonies; by the afternoon, when Ed's case was called, only a few newsmen remained. Our attorneys entered a plea of not guilty on Ed's behalf, asserting that he was innocent of willfully refusing to answer questions that HUAC could not constitutionally ask.

First came four hours of testimony by HUAC attorney Frank Tavenner Jr., speaking for the prosecution. He characterized Ed as a hard-core colonizer of the Communist Party who was sent to the Gary steel mills to organize for the Party.

Next sworn as a witness was Rep. Francis E. Walter, HUAC chair. I was amazed to learn that this was the first time Walter had ever been subpoenaed to testify in a contempt of Congress trial. His appearance made headlines. For an hour and a half—until 9:00 at night—Walter attempted to counter Vic's charge that the aim of HUAC was "exposure for the sake of exposure," an accusation the Supreme Court had acknowledged in the *Watkins* case. To make his point that HUAC actually had no legislative purpose, Vic recited damning statistics: of the 6,580 bills proposed in the first session of the 84th Congress, only one had been referred to HUAC; of the 5,876 bills proposed in the second session, no bills had been referred.

Walter claimed that the legislative purpose of HUAC was "to make people aware of the conspiracy . . . to make people aware of the dangers of Communism."

Vic also charged that HUAC had "high-handedly" denied Ed's

request for an executive session. Queried about the telegrams Vic had sent, Walter denied knowing anything about them until his arrival that very day. The press found Vic's questioning intense: "Rips Walter on Stand in Yellin Trial," said the *Post-Tribune*.

Vic's first witness the next morning was Yale's constitutional historian, Professor Thomas Emerson. After establishing his impressive credentials, Emerson examined the conflict between the needs of an individual and the needs of the government, in light of the *Barenblatt* decision. Government, he explained, "has an interest in seeking information with respect to legislation that will protect against overthrow of the government by force and violence." He examined laws already on the books at the time of the 1958 Gary hearing dealing with matters of internal security: the 1940 Smith Act, which, he said, "prohibited advocacy of overthrow of the government by force and violence"; the 1950 Internal Security Act, which made it illegal "to agree to do any act which substantially contributes to the establishment of a totalitarian dictatorship in the United States" and included "provisions for registration of Communist action and Communist front organizations and for detention camps for use in the event of emergency to incarcerate people whom the Attorney General has reason to believe may engage in sabotage"; and the Communist Control Act, which made it "unlawful for a person to be a member of the Communist Party, knowing the objectives thereof." "The interest of the government in obtaining answers" from a witness "must be weighed in and related to this large mass of legislation dealing with these problems already in existence," he said, in testimony later published in the *Lawyers Guild Review* (Summer 1960).

After noting that the Communist Party had little political influence and that HUAC had already collected testimony at hearings across the country, Emerson then turned to "the interest of the individual in freedom of speech and the interest of society in freedom of speech." He concluded that "the interests of the government in obtaining answers put to this defendant as an aid in developing further legislation to protect internal security are substantially outweighed by the interest of the individual in freedom of speech or silence, as he may prefer, and by the interest of the

community in maintaining freedom of political expression and
other conditions essential to maintaining an open society."

The next day, Judge Swygert ruled Professor Emerson's testimony inadmissible because it was not pertinent to the case, and he
found Ed guilty on four counts of contempt of Congress.

ED

Listening to Judge Swygert declare me guilty, we understood that
he believed that my First Amendment rights were secondary to
the right of the government for self-preservation. This did not surprise us, but hearing him give me the maximum jail sentence for
a misdemeanor—a year in jail for each of the four counts, to be
served concurrently, and a $250 fine—we were astonished.

JEAN

Burton Wechsler, our Gary, Indiana attorney, later told us that
upon hearing the sentence, Vic had turned red and asked to see the
judge in chambers. Burt pleaded with Vic, "Don't do that. I have to
practice here. You're going to leave, but I have to live in this town."
Ignoring him, Vic, who was deeply involved in desegregation strug-
gles, confronted Swygert, noting: "I have conducted these cases all
over the country, in Mississippi and all over the South. I have gone
into the most racist parts of this country and gotten six-month
sentences. You ought to be ashamed of yourself."

Outside the courtroom afterward, speaking to the press, Vic
called Ed's the "harshest sentence" ever imposed in cases of this
kind, and I was quoted as saying the sentence was "shocking." Ed's
only comment was, "I feel confident we can win on appeal."

We knew that most of those convicted of contempt of Congress
had received much smaller penalties. When our attorneys formally
appeared before Judge Swygert on June 17, 1960, in his memorandum to the court requesting a reduction of sentence, Vic summa-
rized a survey of such cases. "In nine," he wrote, "fines and jail sen-

tences were imposed, but the jail sentence at least was suspended. In three more cases, only fines were imposed. All but one or two of these were in the District of Columbia. In six cases, sentences of three months or less were imposed. Three of these were in the District of Columbia. . . . There were nine additional cases in which sentences of four to six months were imposed. Most of these were in the District of Columbia."

His point was that the district court having the greatest amount of experience with these cases had usually suspended sentences or handed out very short jail terms. Furthermore, Vic continued, before Ed's sentencing he knew of only two in which the maximum sentence of a year was imposed: the cases of Carl Braden and Frank Wilkinson, two activists working full-time to defeat HUAC—and they had been sentenced in the District Court of Georgia.

Vic's memo pointed out that Judge Swygert had given two reasons for imposing the maximum sentence: "First, that the defendant had in 1949, when he was 21 years old, filled out an application blank for employment in which he had concealed the extent of his education, and second, that the defendant showed no contrition." Counterposed to this, Vic cited Ed's Ford Foundation Fellowship, awarded after his HUAC appearance, his subsequent reinstatement after his university suspension, and the support he had received from the *St. Louis Post-Dispatch*.

Turning to Swygert's second reason for imposing the maximum sentence, Vic wrote that "the Court misunderstands the reason for the defendant's refusal to answer questions upon the grounds asserted in this case" and that "to expect a show of 'contrition' under these circumstances is unreasonable." He argued that constitutional rights are asserted by some because they think it important to do so even at great personal risk, suggesting that "rights are established only because there are some people who are courageous enough to assert them even when the right has not been widely recognized. Citing examples from the seventeenth century's John Lilburne (who asserted men's "freeborn" rights) to "today's school children in the school desegregation cases," Vic argued that "the issue is not whether they are in fact guilty of violation, but whether they can reasonably be expected to apologize for their struggle."

ED

Vic continued: "Why should he be contrite? . . . The Court may be quite correct in finding him guilty under the law as it sees it, but we must respectfully suggest that it is, in principle, incorrect to expect contrition from a man who is, in good faith, asserting a Constitutional right which he conceives to be important." Noting that some witnesses before HUAC who had asserted their right to plead the Fifth Amendment had been convicted and sentenced but ultimately had their right to avoid self-incrimination upheld by the Supreme Court, Vic pointed out that Ed had made an effort to advance constitutional rights one step further, namely, to establish the right to refuse to answer questions on the basis of the First Amendment. The *Watkins* case seemed to have established that right, and so at Gary "Yellin and three others . . . proceeded in his footsteps. The *Barenblatt* case followed and grave doubt has been cast upon their fight."

JEAN

During Ed's trial, it was rumored in the press that Judge Swygert might be promoted to the empty seat on the Seventh Circuit of the Court of Appeals, to replace Eisenhower-appointee Judge W. Lynn Parkinson, whose neatly folded clothing had been found in October on the shore of Lake Michigan in Chicago, and whose body would be discovered in April. Now our supporters found themselves wondering if Swygert's harsh sentencing of Ed, as well as his judgment against the International Typographers Union the following year, in an early Taft-Hartley case, represented the judge's effort to obtain that vacant seat. If so, he was unsuccessful. Eisenhower selected another man to fill the vacancy, and Swygert would not sit on the Court of Appeals until 1961, when he would be appointed by President John F. Kennedy.

ED

Before my sentencing, Vic had asked Judge Swygert to consider my excellent grades, my marriage, my children, and the heavy debt I had incurred because of the case. Stating that I was trying very, very hard to make a name in the academic field, he requested a suspended sentence.

Judge Swygert found that I "lacked contrition" and gave me the maximum sentence. My comment to the press was, "I feel confident we can win on appeal." But I thought to myself: "$250 is no big deal, but a year in jail! The S.O.B. knew I had more time than money." From then on, what kept me going was a determination to do well in my studies and prove that the bastards couldn't grind me down. "Lacking contrition"? Damn right: I certainly was and will forever remain uncontrite!

JEAN

Soon upon our return to Foley Street, we learned that Ed was all over the local press. Under an eight-column headline, "Here Is What Yellin Told the Committee," the *Champaign-Urbana Courier* used a full page and a half to print the entire transcript of Ed's testimony at the 1958 HUAC hearings. It felt like reading the *New York Times*, not our small-town local paper, and we speculated that the FBI had supplied the *Courier* with the text.

We were big news, and the consequences were immediate! During the recent presidential election, some of our neighbors had voiced such strong anti-Catholic bias against Kennedy that Ed had found himself defending the Vatican. Now, fearing that the flurry of publicity about Ed might cause them concern, I decided to visit the parents of our kids' friends.

When I appeared at the kitchen door of Peter's classmate Ricky, his mother expressed shock and horror at what she had read in the paper about Ed's political past. She professed that it would perhaps be understandable if he "were an embezzler or a bigamist . . . but a Communist!"

Worse was to come, especially for Lisa. Two other little girls lived nearby, and the three children had become inseparable. Daily, hand in hand, they carefully crossed the street from one house to another, then sat together on the lawn busily taking care of their dolls and stuffed animals, parading around playing dress-up, making plans about a birthday party for the summer after kindergarten. Now the mother of one of Lisa's playmates told me that she would not permit our daughter into her house or her daughter into ours. So much for the birthday party that the girls had spent months planning.

When the date arrived, I knew that I needed to get Lisa away and distracted, so I told her that we had to go shopping for her Easter bonnet. No!, she argued. She knew that we never ever went clothes shopping except for the first day of school. She didn't want a new bonnet. She wanted to go to the party.

I couldn't let her stay and see the festivities across the street. I was the mommy, so downtown we went. We didn't come back until dusk, when all of the children had gone home. Fifty years later, Lisa still remembers missing that party, and she remembers the hat. It had a pink ribbon.

CHAPTER FIVE

A Snowball in Hell

JEAN

On March 11, 1960, Ed was found guilty of contempt of Congress. On March 12, after he was sentenced, we went home to Urbana and collected our children from the Bindmans. On March 13, the local paper ran a story, "Yellin's Days as Student Nearing End?" On March 14, Ed was suspended from the graduate college and barred from campus while awaiting a March 22 hearing by a subcommittee on graduate student discipline. Its members were R. W. England Jr., a sociologist; R. W. Touchberry, a geneticist; and Associate Dean Robert M. Sutton. The subcommittee would explore Ed's academic career at all institutions of higher education that he had attended, explore his "activities while employed in Gary for the period" about which HUAC was concerned, and would "feel free to ask the same or similar questions" as HUAC "and any other question relevant to your appearance before that committee."

ED

We discussed the upcoming hearing with our attorney and decided that it would not be advisable to have counsel present. By now I felt mature enough, at thirty-three, to adequately represent myself to the subcommittee, and having an attorney there would set up an undesirably formal and adversarial atmosphere.

Victor Rabinowitz sent a detailed letter to Dean Sutton, informing him and the subcommittee that he was appealing the decision of the district court and that most such cases were ultimately decided in the appellate courts. "It hardly seems necessary to point out that this case does not involve an act of moral turpitude but rather a Constitutional point of considerable significance. . . . In choosing to rely on the First Amendment rather than on the Fifth Amendment, Yellin had made a choice to assert what were, to him, Constitutional rights more important than his own personal security. . . . His conduct in relying on the First Amendment is not an offense of such a nature as to disqualify him as a student at a great university or a teacher in the field of engineering."

On March 19, the student paper, the *Daily Illini*, asked, "What Is Edward Yellin, a Communist or Martyr?" The piece was based on an interview with a reporter who seemed unwilling or unable to answer his own question, concluding, "Depending on the truth or falsity of the charges of Communist activity against him, Yellin's continued consistency in refusing to deny the testimony of his accuser, former FBI undercover agent Joseph LaFleiur [*sic*], is understandable or not so understandable, respectively."

Three days later, the *Daily Illini* had reached a verdict, at least about Ed's suspension: "Yellin is being trapped between the overbearing pressures of public opinion and the public relations attitude of the university. . . . It is conceivable that retaining Yellin could have a disastrous effect on the university especially at this time when the university is fighting to get the large bond issue for education passed. There are people who do not cater to having sons and daughters in the same institution where men refuse to identify past associates and associations. [But] thus far Yellin's most outstanding activity on the Illinois campus has been one of quietly going about acquiring a straight-A average. . . . Until Yellin has exhausted all means of appeal, he should be allowed to remain in school. He has not been convicted of being a Communist; he has been judged guilty of contempt of Congress. But there he was standing on a principle, and if a man cannot do this and remain in the university, there is something drastically wrong with the university's attempt to keep open the avenues of free exchange in the academic marketplace of ideas."

That same day, under the headline "NSA Upholds Yellin's Stand," the paper noted that the chairman of the Illinois chapter of the National Student Association had sent a letter to the Graduate Committee on Discipline stating that "the organization has long maintained that a student's refusal on Constitutional grounds to reply to questions concerning views, affiliations and associations is not just cause for dismissal."

In the five days given me to frame a defense, I scribbled copious notes about the history of HUAC, the factors that had influenced my decision to leave Gary, and "Pertinent Points to Make," which included: "I can truthfully and in good conscience answer questions put to me by this faculty committee. This is not a government agency with the background of the HUAC. . . .

"The issue may not be whether I was right in embarking on a certain course of action, but whether a state institution can afford to defend or tolerate that right.

"I don't feel myself in a position to question the findings of competent scholars that the CP engages in illegal conspiratorial activities, or believes in the overthrow of the government by force and violence. I can only say that I observed no such thing and certainly engaged in no such actions or held such beliefs."

In essence, I had decided that the committee represented the faculty and not the administration, that they were not "out to get me," and that I would be able to engage them in a sincere and honest discussion. I would not only answer all questions asked of me, I would discuss my answers and justify my positions. I was confident that I could convince my interrogators of my sincerity.

I have to admit that I wasn't completely happy with this approach, having lingering questions as to whether it was the most principled course of action. If my political beliefs were protected by the First Amendment, why not stand firm and refuse to submit to questioning by this faculty committee?

I may have too easily backed down. By contrast, Chandler Davis was fired by the University of Michigan when he refused to be interrogated by a faculty committee. That certainly put me to shame!—but he had already finished his doctorate and was able to get a faculty position in Canada. Were I to be expelled as a student, it was very likely that I would find it difficult to finish my graduate studies. No minutes were kept at the hearing, no record of proceedings that could be subpoenaed by HUAC or anyone else. In contrast to my appearance before HUAC, I was completely relaxed and able to engage my questioners in a meaningful discussion. This was possible because I was made to feel that I was not at an inquisition but at an inquiry that was sincerely trying to understand my background and my actions.

A few days afterwards, I wrote another page of notes, "Types of Questions Asked of Me in Hearing." These included: "Queries about CP—when joined? Left? Currently 'on leave of absence?' Did leave CP, go to UM, go to Gary, go to CSU, go to U of I under orders? If disillusioned as 'leader,' why remain in working class? How can an intellectual stay among rank and file so long? Why accept CP position and not word of attorney general? Why falsify employment application? Other applications? Why take 1st? Would I answer questions if FBI asked? If attny general asked? (including naming names). Who is financing case Expenses Hearing and trial? What can offer as an act of faith or think the academic community should be frank and open in discussions?"

The intense press coverage continued. On March 23, the *Courier* printed a piece by James O. Monroe, a member of the state legislature, who said he was writing as "the downstate voice" of the ACLU and condemned the university for my suspension.

JEAN

On March 25, the subcommittee members signed a letter to Ed, stating, "You cooperated fully and your answers to our questions were freely given. . . . We have come to the conclusion that you possess the fitness necessary to continue as a graduate student at the University of Illinois . . . we are, as of this date, recommending your reinstatement."

In an editorial headlined "All Over but the Shouting," the student paper commended the graduate committee for its decision in the face of critics "who will use the university's action as a smear weapon to attack [it] for 'harboring Communists.'" The Champaign-Urbana chapter of the American Association of University Professors also issued a statement denouncing Ed's suspension prior to the inquiry as "provocative" but hailing the university for being "faithful to the highest American standards of due process."

At home, what we felt was physical relief. Ed had shed about ten pounds during his suspension. The newspaper photo of him making a triumphant phone call to his mother shows a rather gaunt young man. Now he rushed back to campus to make up two weeks of lost academics.

ED

Upon my return to campus, my office mates made no comments, and consistent with my desire to not let the case dominate my life, I chose not to initiate any discussion. Only one faculty member commented, while he and I were at neighboring urinals: "It must be tough for you to catch up your missing classes." His friendly smile and tone of voice made me feel supported.

JEAN

I found the events of that spring—the trial, the sentencing, the suspension, the reinstatement—difficult to absorb. Aware of the publicity surrounding Ed's case, I also judged it certain that I would not be rehired by the local board of education.

So I went back to school. I searched for an English course given at 8:00 a.m. so I could attend and run back home in time for Ed to get to his office not too much after and still get in a full day's work. I had not been in a classroom for years; I had been talking mostly with babies and toddlers. Contrary to my expectations, however, I was apparently not the oldest student in the room. Summer session, I learned, was an opportunity for high school teachers to earn

additional credits toward an advanced degree, so I was surrounded by them.

Five mornings a week, I listened to Professor Ed Davidson use words that I had never heard before (which I attempted to spell phonetically beyond the red margin line down the left side of my notebook). Learning of my distress at my limited vocabulary, which I feared prevented me from adequate classroom participation, a classmate shared the reassuring information that this professor was known to keep himself alert by learning new words each

day and using them in his lectures. Nobody knew what they meant, and nobody cared.

As it happened, Professor Davidson liked to teach summer school at 8:00 because the lecture room didn't become unbearably hot until somewhat later in the morning. His field was American literature. An extremely civil man, he planned small conferences with each of his students. Working methodically through the alphabet, he arranged to meet with me in late summer, after I had written several short papers. During our talk, he suggested that perhaps I would like to become a teaching assistant. When I demurred, explaining that I had never taken anything called "Freshman English," he said that was really no problem and pointed out that I was older than most students and should be able to manage.

Clearly, one could not become a graduate assistant unless one was enrolled as a graduate student. Thus began my academic career. Interestingly, it did not occur to me at the time—or, indeed, during my years in Urbana—that in light of the huge publicity Ed was receiving in the local press, it was a bold move for Professor Davidson to recruit me. Neither he nor I ever mentioned it.

I found it fun to read and reread Herman Melville and the Transcendentalists, especially Henry David Thoreau. To my ears, his injunction, "Become the friction that stops the machine," really resonated. I felt that he was speaking directly to Ed and me. I read it again and again.

At the same time that spring, we had been trying to create a support system, asking various individuals and organizations to protest Ed's conviction and send letters to the press and the university to protest his suspension, and later to congratulate the school for his reinstatement. In Chicago, Dick Criley of the Committee to Defend Democratic Rights wrote to the *Sun-Times* and the *Tribune*; the Essex Community Church's Reverend William T. Baird alerted his supporters to Ed's situation; and the *Nation*'s Cary McWilliams wrote a personal letter to university president David Henry.

The most significant support came from Irving Dilliard's editorial, "Between Two Decisions," published in the *St. Louis Post-Dispatch* shortly after Ed's reinstatement. Applauding the university's decision, Dilliard explained that Ed had refused to answer HUAC's questions "on the ground that the committee was infringing upon his freedom of speech and thought without legislative purpose." Asking why he was not indicted until a year after his contempt citation, the editorial pointed out that Ed had based his 1958 refusal on the 1957 U. S. Supreme Court's decision in the *Watkins* case, which had found that HUAC "had asked questions not pertinent to a clear legislative intent of Congress." Dilliard also quoted the Court's decision: "There is no congressional power to expose for the sake of exposure." Pointing out that the government did not prosecute Ed until after the 1959 *Barenblatt* decision, which retreated from *Watkins* to rule, 5–4, that "that the committee's authority was 'unassailable'," the editorial concluded, "Mr. Yellin is the victim of legal uncertainties left by two decisions, one of which the second held to be incorrect."

Concerning Ed's suspension, the piece noted that State Senator James O. Monroe had issued "a vigorous statement" on behalf of "academic freedom" and that the university subcommittee had found that Yellin was ready to answer the questions he had refused to answer for HUAC. It concluded: "Under the rule of the McCarthy period Mr. Yellin might have been dismissed outright. Instead, the University of Illinois deserves great credit for avoiding inflexible judgment of a scholar who claimed freedom of conscience." Reading this, we felt strengthened.

Dilliard's editorial was republished in the *Courier* and the *Illini*, and was instrumental in gaining us local support. We created a collage of Ed's press clippings and sent it out to supporters and to all of the civil liberties organizations we could think of: the American Civil Liberties Union and its Illinois branch; the Rights of Conscience Committee of the American Friends Service Committee; Frank Wilkerson's Citizens Committee to Defend Democratic Rights; the National Lawyers Guild; the Committee of First Amendment Defendants; and the Emergency Civil Liberties Committee.

We asked these organizations for money to help with our legal expenses, and proposed that they write an amicus brief supporting the argument we were planning to make before the Supreme Court. Although none of the organizations sent money or agreed to write a brief, a number of them reported that they were providing briefs in other First Amendment cases and wished us well.

When we read that Rep. James Roosevelt, standing on the floor of the House of Representatives, had proposed the abolition of HUAC—quoting Rep. Walter's testimony at Ed's trial—and that Roosevelt had initially voted against formation of the Committee because he thought its function should be within the jurisdiction of the House Judiciary Committee, and still thought so—we believed that we really might have hurried the demise of HUAC.

We fully endorsed Roosevelt's quotation of his mother Eleanor's criticism of HUAC (July 12, 1959) that it had become "an agency for the destruction of human dignity and Constitutional rights."

ED

For a half century, Jean and I believed that Fred Wall, dean of the graduate school, had played a villainous role and stolen ten days of my education and threatened my future. In 2012, while doing research in the University of Illinois archive for this book, we learned what had happened behind the scenes. The archive revealed that in 1963, Dean Wall had written a nineteen-page report on my situation at the university. In it, Wall recalled that on Thanksgiving weekend, 1959, he had received a phone call from a faculty member of the American Association of University Professors asking what the graduate college would do to a graduate student who, on the basis of the First Amendment, had refused to answer questions at a HUAC hearing and had been indicted for contempt of Congress. Wall had replied that the school would do nothing pending the outcome of a trial.

At the time of my trial, Wall's report continued, a number of items in the newspaper caused "a flurry of activity" and "sporadic suggestions that I be dismissed." A couple of weeks earlier, Wall had attended a meeting where, with several university officials present, it was suggested that "drastic action be taken." Jealous of intrusion into graduate college affairs, he had maintained that if there were any action, it had to come from the graduate college. Hearing predictions that I would be found guilty, he continued: "the proper steps . . . had to be taken before any graduate student could be dismissed." At the conclusion of the trial but before any decision was taken, it was decided that if I were found guilty, I should neither be "summarily dismissed nor assured of continuation in the Graduate College, but he should have a hearing."

Dean Wall wrote that because of prior professional commitments, he had been away from campus during my trial, but it had been decided that if he were not in Urbana if and when the judge pronounced a guilty verdict, an associate dean would suspend me and arrange for a hearing before an appropriate committee. "We reasoned that by suspending Yellin we could, on the one hand, assure the radical right that we meant business, and, on the other hand, get the liberals to cooperate in granting a quick hearing."

Immediately upon arriving in California, Wall wrote, he heard by phone that I had indeed been found guilty and had been suspended, "but there were rumblings about procedures. There were some pressures to dismiss Yellin immediately. . . . The upshot . . . was that we would observe procedures to the letter of the university statutes." Wall had charged the subcommittee "to conduct the inquiry in the fairest manner . . . without prejudice and especially without taking cognizance of any outside pressures, whether they arose by letter, newspaper articles, or otherwise," and he had assured the subcommittee, "I would defend their recommendation and stand by the decision."

His report continued, "It is difficult to say for sure what might have happened if the suspension had not been invoked, but I question whether Yellin would have been permitted to continue as a student if some such plan had not been put into effect."

Interestingly, in 1991, more than three decades after my Illinois suspension and reinstatement, Fred Wall, now retired from academia, voiced a somewhat different view. In an interview for the Chemical Heritage Foundation's Oral History Program, surveying his long professional career, he recalled his response to my conviction for contempt of Congress: "I resented what was going on when I read in the newspapers that the administration was seriously thinking about throwing Yellin out of school. I made it clear that if anybody was going to throw him out of school, I was the one to do it. Not that I wanted to throw him out of school, but I didn't want somebody else to step in and encroach on my responsibilities. . . .

"I realized that if I left town to deliver my scheduled lectures the president would almost surely find some way to throw the guy out during my absence. The question was what I should do. What I did was to compromise in a sense. I suspended Yellin. I didn't throw him out, but I suspended him pending investigation. That took the immediate heat off because no one could say I had done nothing.

"I did not come out looking very good to many liberals. They said I was wishy-washy, but I can now assert that Yellin wouldn't have had the chance of a snowball in hell when I was gone, because I knew enough about how the university functioned. I put him, you might say, in protective custody. . . .

"Subsequently, I talked with him. He was grateful for the fact that I had reinstated him. I doubt that he was pleased that I had suspended him, but I told him as much as I reasonably could."

Almost immediately after my reinstatement, President David D. Henry did summarily throw someone out of the university—a professor of biology who had written a letter to the student paper defending premarital sex and trial marriage for "mature adults." Calling Leo Koch's ideas offensive and repugnant, Henry fired him without following any normal academic procedures.

JEAN

In 1960, we had had no idea of the pressures Fred Wall had felt when he suspended Ed. We had no clue that by insisting on appropriate academic procedures, Wall was knowingly flying in the face of powerful forces within the university and endangering his own professional future. We didn't understand that in appointing a graduate disciplinary committee, he felt that he was putting Ed into "protective custody," not only to protect Ed but also to protect himself from the wrath of the Red-haters, who, he wrote, "couldn't say I had done nothing."

It was not until 1991—after Fred Wall had retired from his profession and more than thirty years after the event—that he attested to the poisonous atmosphere at the university in 1960.

Wall explained that in consequence of his decision to follow the academic procedures that saved Ed's chance at a professional life, he was punished a year or two later when "there was a general university budget increase with widespread salary increases . . . practically every administrator except me" received a raise. "The message," he knew, "was clear." As a result, he left Illinois and spent the balance of his career at the University of California.

Even a man highly placed in the academy could not defy the strictures of the House Un-American Activities Committee without punishment. Only decades later did we learn of the professional pressures Wall had felt when, suddenly confronted by McCarthyism, he had followed his conscience and defied pressure, thereby altering his entire career.

We knew that our family was unhappy living through these tribulations in the hostile Foley Street neighborhood, so as soon as the children's school year ended, we moved into student housing. In Urbana, that meant rebuilt barracks—certainly not as nice as our three-bedroom rental on Foley Street. We had several friends that lived there, however, and we believed that living among students would provide a safer, friendlier place to raise our children. Sadly, we had to give up Blintz, because dogs were not allowed in Stadium Terrace student housing. Reluctantly, we took him back to the shelter and moved on. Buying buckets of white paint at Sears, Ed and I went round and round the tiny rooms, adding layers and layers of paint until whatever was underneath could no longer be seen.

I had fun writing my first papers on American literature. Parsing Thoreau's injunction to stop the machine was more challenging than keeping up with our growing defense committee correspondence. While Ed was writing to professional societies concerning materials he hoped to use to teach an engineering course in the fall, and to his faculty advisor and to members of the graduate college subcommittee thanking them for their confidence, and to the editors of the *Nation* and *St. Louis Post-Dispatch* in gratitude for their meaningful support during his suspension, I was typing thank-you notes to supporters. With all five of us in school, the family was settling into our new life.

But our sensational year at the University of Illinois was not yet over. Champaign-Urbana citizens awoke one morning to the news that two graduate math students, William Martin and Bernon Mitchell, had just appeared on Russian television. Declaring that they feared a nuclear war and had defected to the Soviet Union, they denounced several U.S. policies as provocative, and cited American incursions into the air space of other nations and spying on America's allies. HUAC immediately labeled them "sex deviants." And suddenly the Illinois campus was swarming with FBI agents—who were totally uninterested in Ed.

It was a relief that we had never met either Martin or Mitchell.

CHAPTER SIX

In Lieu of "Ability"

JEAN

We had reason to be joyful when Ed, after sitting for a competitive exam, learned in March 1961 that he had won a $3,800 fellowship from the National Science Foundation (NSF). The NSF had been charged by Congress to grant fellowships "solely on the basis of ability," and although soon enough Ed received a phone call from someone at the Foundation asking about the status of his case in the courts and verifying that he planned to appeal to the Supreme Court, we assumed that all was well.

The NSF was created during the Cold War in 1950. Seven years later, the Soviet Union launched *Sputnik*, the first human-made Earth satellite, and the space race was on, with Congress passing the National Defense Education Act, which poured billions into the U.S. educational system to train a new generation of engineers, scientists, and physicists to compete with the Soviets. The National Defense Education Act did not require that fellowship applicants be saddled with full FBI investigations, but it did include a mandate that they sign an oath and affidavit patterned on those required for NSF fellowships, which disclaimed belief in the overthrow of the government.

ED

On June 8, 1961, in a *Congressional Record* item headlined "Communist Subversion of the United States from Within," HUAC member Gordon Scherer (R-Ohio) attacked my fellowship, along with the National Science Foundation, the University of Illinois, and John F. Kennedy's White House. Scherer proclaimed himself "shocked and sickened" that I—"whose conviction for contempt of Congress for refusal to testify concerning his Communist activities within basic industry was recently affirmed by the U.S. Seventh Circuit Court of Appeals"—had won a fellowship. Scherer charged NSF with "a conspiracy of silence or an unwillingness to take even the most casual look at Yellin's background." Further, he objected that "on instructions from the White House" NSF officials refused to furnish HUAC with "the recommendations of the officials of the University of Illinois that Yellin be granted this fellowship."

Within days, the chair of the NSF's parent House Committee on Science and Astronautics, Rep. Overton Brooks (D-LA), announced being "shocked that the Foundation granted an award to a man previously convicted of refusing to answer questions put to him by the House Committee on Un-American Activities."

The press was quick to pounce. In a June 14 editorial headed "Preposterous Perversion of Justice: Scholarship Aid to Communists," the *St. Louis Globe-Democrat* condemned my fellowship: "Government policy of giving aid, financial or otherwise, to enemies of the state is a preposterous perversion of justice. . . . We are simply living in a fool's world if we feel that untrustworthy and traitorous scientists are an advantage to America. . . . There always remains the possibility that an Edward Yellin . . . . could turn into a [atomic spy like] Klaus Fuchs."

Another member of the Committee on Science and Astronautics, Richard L. Roudebush (R-IN), demanded an investigation, saying he was amazed, appalled, and, frankly, downright angry. NSF director Alan T. Waterman was ordered to appear before the committee at 10:00 a.m. on June 15—and to appear before HUAC two hours earlier! He thus found himself the subject of a congressional tug-of-war over the race to revoke my fellowship.

JEAN

For two days, the Committee on Science and Astronautics tried to solve the problem created by Ed's award. Their difficulty was that NSF was mandated by Congress to grant fellowships "solely on the basis of ability." "Consequently," wrote the *St. Louis Globe-Democrat*, "when Director Waterman was asked if the Foundation would have awarded [the] fellowship if they had known about [Ed's] conviction for contempt of Congress, he answered, 'I believe so.' This response angered Rep. Anfuso (D-NY), who asked if Waterman thought Ed Yellin's 'ability' had not been impaired by his conviction for 'this most heinous crime.' Although Rep. Charles A. Mosher (R-OH) wished that [Yellin] had not received the award, he thought that 'an even greater mistake would be made . . . if we gave the public . . . and the scientific and academic community the impression that whenever an individual gives an unpopular opinion or signs an unpopular petition he seriously risks his scientific career.'"

Chairman Brooks reported that the NSF counsel told him he was attempting to determine whether the NSF could legally revoke the fellowship. Discovering that NSF applications included faculty recommendations, the committee clamored to examine the four Illinois faculty members who had endorsed Ed's application. At first Waterman refused to reveal their identities, arguing that the academic community would feel threatened by government interference. On the second day of hostile questioning, however, he named the four who had acted as Ed's references.

Both congressional committees were eager to investigate them. In his opening *Congressional Record* tirade, Rep. Scherer attacked the NSF's initial efforts to avoid naming them: "These professors are no more part of the Executive Branch than the man in the moon." Shortly afterwards, the Science and Astronautics Committee revealed that an investigator might be sent to Illinois to question them.

ED

Back in Urbana, my advisor, Professor Seichi Konzo, trying to head them off, detailed the NSF fellowship application process to a *Chicago Tribune* reporter. Faculty members, he explained, were routinely expected to fill out forms for students. He stated that after questioning, I had assured him that I could sign the required loyalty oath without hesitation, and that—in light of my reinstatement at the university, which had concluded that I "should be treated as a bona fide student"—Konzo had filled out a standard application form for me. He added, "It should be made clear that this is not a reference in the usual sense. It is essentially a rating form rather than an expression of opinions."

JEAN

We could not believe what we were reading in the newspapers. One of Ed's references had been signed by his department chair, Helmut H. Korst, an Austrian scientist who had worked for Adolf Hitler's war machine before emigrating to the U.S. after World War II. Under the headline "Korst Denies Endorsement of Yellin," the professor was quoted by the *News Gazette* as saying that to call the forms "references" was "either the result of lack of facts or distortion." They were, he asserted, only "simple sheets of paper with little boxes on them. By checking the proper boxes we hope to give a fair appraisal of a student's academic worth. . . . There is no provision on the form," he added, "for any personal judgment and it is certainly not a letter of recommendation." A few days later, responding to Rep. Scherer's threat that the university act against him and the other professors, Korst demanded a letter of apology from Scherer. Announcing that he shared HUAC's effort to deal effectively with national security, he wrote that the professors Scherer had attacked "were not asked for recommendations nor endorsement of a person. . . . To insinuate that filling out scholastic rating forms constitutes an 'endorsement' of the applicant is as baseless as to claim that giving a grade in a course approves of a student's moral conduct."

ED

Decades later, we were able to examine those "simple sheets of paper." It is true that on one side they have only "little boxes on them." On the other side, however, all four referees wrote comments in the space the forms provided.

While the issue of faculty recommendations was absorbing Champaign-Urbana, Rep. Francis E. Walter (D-PA), the chair of HUAC who had testified at my trial, issued in the "Case of Edward Yellin and the National Science Foundation," a stinging attack on NSF director Waterman. He accused the director of "evading his obvious responsibility" and "passing the buck" because, instead of terminating my fellowship, Waterman had referred the application to the Department of Justice to determine whether or not I had perjured myself by signing the NSF oath and affidavit. Beyond doubt, Walter wrote, Ed Yellin was identified as a member of the Communist Party and one of its colonizers in the steel industry. Now, "even as he applies for a government handout, he continues in his failure to make known to the government the identity of enemy agents who may be working today as colonizers in an industry which is vital to our defense effort. . . . If all government officials were as disinterested as Waterman in America's security," Walter concluded, "our security would be a horrible mess."

Director Waterman sent me a telegram that morning: "We regret to advise you that after a full review of all the facts in your situation, including the possibility that you may not be able to pursue your studies without interruption during the fellowship tenure, the present fellowship award made to you on March 15 for 1961–62 is revoked."

Many years later, we learned that Waterman was hoping he had sent that wire before he was denounced by HUAC. In 1991, I received a letter from J. Merton England, who identified himself as the retired historian of the National Science Foundation. To complete an unfinished account of NSF history, he was requesting my opinion of an article he was writing about the end of NSF's disclaimer affidavit. The center of the piece, he explained, would deal with my fellowship application and its aftermath. I replied favorably, a pleasant correspondence followed, and in time I received England's manuscript and its published version.

England located the history of the revocation of my NSF fellowship within the larger context of the struggle to end loyalty oaths—both the one required by the NSF and the one incorporated into the National Defense Education Act. Reading England's references, I saw mention of a "Diary Note" among NSF director Waterman's papers, and wrote to the National Archives asking for a copy. I promptly received a Xerox of the handwritten note, which read (verbatim): "Question: what would NSF do re this case if facts known earlier—In general NSF will grant no fellowship to criminals—However crime might be relevant to ability eg perjury, murder and other felonies—no criminal negligence manslaughter ( ) What about final appeal ATW this case Univ of Ill hearing Candidate loyal, able, serious (?)"

In a cover letter, the National Archives informed me that their Yellin files included approximately 115 pages, and asked whether I would like to see them. Absolutely! In a brief time, I received two compact discs containing NSF's internal notes and correspondence about me.

JEAN

And so, more than thirty years later, we learned a lot more about the National Science Foundation and the "Yellin Case." The situation was summed up by NSF director Waterman in his notes for the meeting of the NSF executive committee on June 19, 1961: "The Yellin case is, of course, a most serious matter not only for the NSF but for national policy."

One of Waterman's notes reports that following Congressman Scherer's June 8 attack on the Foundation, and just two days after the June 18 announcement by Rep. Brooks expressing shock that a man convicted of refusing to answer HUAC's questions was awarded a NSF fellowship, NSF general counsel William J. Hoff had drafted a memo to the Foundation executive committee: "Under the present statute we have little basis for taking into account conviction for a crime or the commission of acts which do not demonstrably reflect upon ability, although we certainly could provide by rule that the question of ability to pursue the courses of studies outlined for the term involved was a prerequisite to receive the award."

We learned that Ed had been the focus of the agenda for the June 19, 1961, NSF executive committee meeting: "Can and should we enlarge considerations entering into ability?" "What action should be taken on the Yellin fellowship?" "Does conviction of contempt of Congress affect his 'ability'?" "What weight should be attached to the fact that his case has been appealed to the Supreme Court?" "Does the fact that his tenure may be interrupted by a jail sentence warrant suspending the fellowship?"

In an administratively restricted memo, attorney Hoff reminded executive committee members that the Foundation was to award fellowships "solely on the basis of ability."

To deal with Ed, efforts to define "ability" now became grotesque. Hoff proposed that an "applicant's 'ability' clearly would include such aspects of character and performance as could fairly be said to have a relationship to the successful completion of his studies and his future work," but if the board decided that "membership in the Communist Party in the U.S. today shows such allegiance to foreign discipline as to reflect adversely upon the ability of the candidate, this could be a factor in the selection process." Further, said Hoff, if the board believed that "refusal to cooperate with a Congressional investigating committee, as proven by subsequent conviction for contempt of Congress, has a relationship to an applicant's scientific ability or scientific integrity, then again this could be made a matter to be considered."

It might become necessary, he continued, to categorize crimes: "Perhaps a conviction of perjury would reflect upon professional ability, whereas a conviction for criminal negligence, for instance, for leaving a swimming pool unguarded, might not be considered to reflect on ability. Somewhere in between these two will be a dividing line but, in my opinion, it is almost impossible to categorize crimes and say that one affects ability and another does not." Hoff thought it impossible for the NSF "to sort out crimes on the basis of whether or not they materially reflect on ability, and, therefore, if such matters are to be considered, I would be inclined to favor a policy of not awarding fellowships where anything is likely to interfere with the tenure of the fellowship."

In short, he had found a solution to NSF's "Yellin problem"—if Ed were in jail, he would not be able to serve out the tenure of the fellowship.

Still, the question of "ability" continued to absorb the NSF. A June 24 memorandum to members of the National Science Board addressed the subject: "The Foundation has always judged that the term 'ability' includes, in addition to intellectual ability, the accepted requisition for sound scientific research or teaching, namely, motivation, independence and objectivity of judgment, accuracy and, especially, integrity." In addition, "conviction of a crime casting doubt on the loyalty or integrity of an individual . . . can reflect on his ability to perform his subsequent teaching or research activities."

ED

Examining the National Science Foundation papers, we were amazed to find correspondence leading us directly to Kennedy's White House. In a memo on June 7, 1961, Lee C. White, assistant special counsel to the president, informed Kennedy that he advised that the NSF make my fellowship application available to HUAC, but that revealing the responses of the four faculty references included in the application presented problems: "The Chairman was advised that they were received in confidence, and more importantly, that if divulged, the ability of the NSF to secure frank and candid evaluations of applicants would be seriously impaired." Therefore, White continued, the HUAC chairman was told he could see the papers personally on an "eyes only" basis. White suggested to Kennedy that if HUAC rejected this, "I recommend that you exercise the right of executive privilege and direct the NSF to withhold the four documents" because "the howls from academic and liberal quarters would be deafening." The next day, White reported to Kennedy, "We have advised the NSF to suspend or withdraw an NSF scholarship awarded to Edward Yellin."

JEAN

It was almost two weeks later, on June 21, that Rep. Walter unleashed his fierce attack on Waterman, who wired Ed revoking his fellowship. On that same day, Waterman also made a diary note labeled personal and confidential, which recorded his phone call to Rep. Brooks, chair of the House Committee on Science and Astronautics, assuring him that he had terminated Ed's fellowship and "called in the Executive Board and talked it over." Considering changes needed in NSF fellowship applications to prevent another situation like Ed's, Waterman feared that "we would antagonize the scientists by the idea of having investigations for everybody." When he reported to Brooks that he had been in touch with the White House, Brooks responded that he was "sure that the Chief would approve of anything that struck at the communists."

That was a busy day for Waterman. He also phoned Jerome Wiesner, special assistant to the president for science and technology, telling him about Walter's attack and reporting that he had informed Brooks about the revocation of Ed's fellowship. Waterman then phoned the assistant counsel to the president, Lee J. White, to tell him that he had revoked the fellowship and spoken with Brooks. Discussing Walter's personal attack on him, Waterman wrote that "the telegram [to Ed] was sent about eleven o'clock and the blast from . . . Walter was released about one o'clock, I understand. . . . Mr. White said he hoped the sequence was in order."

The diary entry noted that White had told Waterman that Kennedy had said "it would be good to act before anybody absolutely demanded that it be done. Mr. White added that he was glad we beat their blast. . . . I told him that the first I knew of the release by Walters [*sic*] was when someone handed it to me about 3:30 p.m. today." It is unclear whether, as Waterman hoped, he had managed to revoke the fellowship before being attacked by Walter, but the deed was done.

ED

Immediately after I received Waterman's telegram, I reached my lawyer, Victor Rabinowitz, who wrote to the NSF board requesting that the revocation be taken up by the entire body at their upcoming meeting. Voicing his "complete confidence in the soundness" of my appeal to the Supreme Court, he asserted, "there is no justification for the Foundation assuming anything to the contrary," and he questioned Waterman's authority to revoke the fellowship.

JEAN

What I recall most clearly about that week is that I did a lot of typing. I was copying the two-page, single-spaced letter that Ed had quickly composed asking for an opportunity to defend himself, which I typed individually and sent to each of the twenty-five board members, some of whom were the most prominent scientists in the country—including the presidents of the Rockefeller Institute, MIT, and Cal Tech, the president of research at Bell Labs, and the board chair at Abbott Labs. Writing that "my integrity has been impugned . . . my loyalty has been questioned, and . . . my professional future has been endangered," Ed voiced distress that neither Congress nor the National Science Board has seen fit to include me in its deliberations" and petitioned each board member to consider the restitution of his fellowship at their June 28 meeting. The letter pointed out that Waterman had made the decision to revoke Ed's fellowship after consulting with only five members instead of the entire executive board, as required.

An invitation to meet with the executive board never came.

Decades later, reading the NSF files, we learned that only one man had responded to his plea. According to Waterman's notes, on June 28, board member Professor Paul M. Gross of Duke University phoned, saying that he had received Ed's request to consider restoring the fellowship. This was merely a suggestion, Gross noted, but "a hearing is a good American practice."

CHAPTER SEVEN

Uncompromising Independence

JEAN

The National Science Foundation's scrapping of Ed's fellowship triggered national publicity in the summer of 1961. "Subversion and Education" was the headline *Science* used (June 23, 1961) to alert the scientific community to the revocation of his fellowship. After recounting President Kennedy's repeated efforts to repeal the requirement that a college student receiving a government loan sign an affidavit disclaiming subversive beliefs and affiliations, the article reported on the hearings of the House Committee on Science and Astronautics that charged the National Science Foundation with being "lax from the standpoint of security" in awarding Ed's fellowship.

The next week, *Science*'s lead editorial, "One in Eighteen Thousand," stated that both HUAC and the Science and Astronautics Committee had questioned NSF officials about Ed, and that the NSF executive committee had revoked his fellowship. Reflecting the historic concern of scientists when government intrudes into scientific affairs, the editorial commented that opinion about the wisdom of this action is divided. According to one view, the fellowship might have been suspended to give time for a careful consideration of policy to govern this and future cases. The policy question is: "Is conviction for a criminal offense adequate grounds for denying or revoking a fellowship? The law governing fellowships says that they shall be awarded 'solely on the basis of ability.'" The editorial then suggested a "simple remedy": that the NSF include on its application form a question about the candidate's criminal record. "Some crimes," it concluded, "are more relevant than others."

That same issue of *Science*, reporting a congressional demand for changes in the NSF Act "to prevent the award of a grant to a student of questionable loyalty," announced a bill by Rep. Brooks that would write into law "the interpretation of 'ability' which the Foundation used as part of the basis for rescinding Yellin's grant." The bill, it reported, "appeared extremely likely to pass."

In July, *Scientific American* reviewed Ed's situation in its column, "The Citizen Scientist." Its comment was in its title: "In Lieu of Ability."

In September, the *Bulletin of Atomic Scientists* published a detailed summary of Ed's situation, suggesting the possibility that "the ostensible reason for revoking the fellowship was to avoid an inconvenient conflict with some elements in Congress and the press."

The national press weighed in. In a strong editorial, "Succumbing to Pressure," the *St. Louis Post-Dispatch* rebuked Waterman for caving in "so easily to congressional criticism on the Yellin case . . . it was not very courageous, to say the least, to withdraw the fellowship merely because of congressional pressure. . . . We cannot believe the security of the United States would be jeopardized meanwhile by Mr. Yellin pursuing his studies in his chosen field."

In the *New York Herald-Tribune*, Robert C. Toth wrote, "There have been suggestions that the 33-year-old Yellin was made a scapegoat by the National Science Foundation to head off congressional action on its programs and those of other Administration agencies." Toth reported that the NSF was "deeply concerned" that a bill before Congress adding additional loyalty requirements on government fellowships would have "serious repercussions in the nation's scientific community." The "Yellin Case," he explained, has been discussed in the White House because of its implications concerning both the government's overall education policy and government efforts to remove the loyalty oath from the National Education Act, while making the program permanent.

The proposed bill, sponsored by Rep. Brooks, chair of the House

Science Committee, would, Toth continued, award fellowships not "solely on ability," but "on the basis of character, ability and loyalty to the United States and its Constitutional form of government." The bill would also require an applicant to sign an affidavit concerning whether he had ever been "arrested, charged, or held" for law violations—excluding traffic offenses.

In August, the *Detroit News* headlined an article, "OK Bill to Bar Reds on Science Scholarships." A month later, trumpeting its support of a bill by HUAC's Rep. Walter that made it illegal for Communists to apply for an NSF grant, the *St. Louis Globe-Democrat* blustered, "if there is a great, grassroots dissatisfaction over Washington's 'softness' toward Communism, it is because of the kind of attitude displayed in the Yellin case."

ED

I had eagerly anticipated strong support from the scientific community—and there was a little. In *Science*, one letter writer commented thatthe June editorial endorsing the revocation of the fellowship was "the first time that I have found an idea proposed by an editor of *Science* so repugnant and outrageous. . . . Including a question on the NSF application without conviction for a crime is one more manifestation of a trend in present-day society to suggest, and sometimes even to accept, protestations and oaths of loyalty, purity, and moral righteousness in place of such qualities as capability, originality, and creative thought."

Another letter, arguing that the central issue in my case was "freedom of the individual conscience and the privacy of ideas," concluded that "protection of freedom of thought is particularly important to us as scientists. It would be harmful to all of us if political clearance became a necessary condition to obtaining a federally supported fellowship."

There was, however, no widespread condemnation of the revocation of the NSF grant. As I wrote to fellow HUAC victim Chandler Davis, "I feel that the lack of open, concerted, and national support against the action of the NSF was extremely disheartening."

Throughout the NSF crisis, I got in touch with numerous colleagues, including Gerard Piel, editor of *Scientific American*, whom
I asked for "some knowledgeable opinions and advice on what I
may expect in the way of opportunities for both study and future
employment." A month later, I wrote again (September 30, 1961):
"I am in the midst of writing to distinguished investigators in the
field of cardiovascular research in hopes of getting into a training
program, or becoming involved as a research assistant. While this
might seem to be a useless task, it is being done at the suggestion
of Dr. Peters, the director of medical research for the American
Heart Association. He feels that any university worth its salt, if it
feels my ability merits, will give me money and stand up to Washington. In addition, these letters will establish some useful contacts from whom to solicit advice and information in the future."

JEAN

The publicity about Ed's situation also triggered his correspondence with Chandler Davis, a Harvard-trained mathematician who
had been fired four years earlier from the University of Michigan
for refusing to answer HUAC's questions. Davis had grounded his
refusal on the First Amendment, and in 1960 had served a six-
month jail sentence for contempt of Congress. Following Ed's situation in the press, Davis introduced himself: "You're in the same
stranded state I was in for some months in 1954. . . . HUAC, in
deliberately setting out to make it impossible for ideas of the left
to be heard by the public . . . is violating the spirit of the Preamble
and First Amendment . . . its proceedings being unconstitutional
exercise of government power. . . . therefore it is not possible to
commit contempt of Congress at these proceedings."

Acknowledging the probability that Ed's conviction would be
upheld by the Supreme Court, Davis turned to practical advice
about prison, cautioning Ed: "It's a drag, but it's not intolerable;
it won't exalt you, but it won't corrupt you . . . and may enlighten
you." He continued, "Don't ask any warden ANYTHING until you
are in his prison temporarily; the warden doesn't give a damn

about you. Once you have a number, he may still not give a LARGE damn, but you are his responsibility. . . . Keep your eyes open, ask questions judiciously, don't pester people."

ED

I wrote back to Chandler Davis that my attorney did not plan to base his argument before the Supreme Court on classic First Amendment grounds, but on the *Barenblatt* decision's doctrine of "balancing," and would seek to show that the "balance" should be struck in my favor. "This is certainly a retreat from principle since the balancing doctrine is in itself a violation of the First Amendment. However, coming as it does after Barenblatt, Davis, Braden and Wilkenson [sic] [all First Amendment defendants who had been jailed], there does not seem much hope to win on straight First Amendment grounds. From now on, a reverse on a technicality is a victory."

I added: "I have avoided placing my extra-legal defense on organizations . . . because I do not think they would conduct a campaign which would reach and influence new people. The result has been that we have had to do it all ourselves."

Yet we certainly tried to involve others in my case. The students who had responded to my suspension and reinstatement now protested the revocation of my NSF fellowship. Organizing themselves into the Champaign-Urbana Committee on the "Yellin Case," they issued a press release asserting that "Yellin's work in bio-medical engineering does not involve the national security . . . nor has he been proven a 'Communist or subversive,' as some members of Congress have implied. The cancellation of the grant indicates that the NSF has bowed to political pressure." They also sent a fact sheet to alumni and began visiting faculty to urge them to persuade the university to support my work during the upcoming academic year.

Scratching around for more help, we discovered the Quakers, who graciously welcomed us to their weekly potluck dinners, providing not only food but a social space where we could decompress with our children, six-year-old Michael, seven-year-old Lisa, and ten-year-old Peter.

JEAN

Throughout, Ed was attending classes and earning straight A's, while I worked as a teaching assistant and became more and more seriously involved in the study of American literature. Despite all of the pressures and publicity, I didn't feel embarrassed or even particularly conspicuous, although I was, some days, meeting my freshman rhetoric class with Ed's name all over the front page of the *Daily Illini*, tucked next to the textbook under my arm.

One incident, however, did feel awkward. I was at home with the kids in the late afternoon when I answered a knock at the door. A young man introduced himself as Dan Perlmutter, a new faculty member, who had come to give us money. He explained that he was one of a group of friends who had read about our plight and decided to help. He had accepted the assignment of calling on us with their donation.

I really didn't know how to accept the help, and he didn't really know how to offer it, but somehow the task was accomplished, and when Ed came home, I gave him my amazed report. That was a lifetime ago. In the decades since, we have become close to Dan and their family, living links to our difficult Illinois days.

ED

We were reaching out in a dozen directions that summer. We needed to reach the scientific community to convince the NSF to reinstate my grant (although this surely was unlikely). We needed to reach Illinois students, faculty, and alums to persuade the university to somehow find something—an assistantship? a fellowship?—that would enable me to continue my studies (although the administration had declared that this was impossible). Lacking an academic income, we needed to try to identify a patron who would provide support.

In addition, I needed to identify a scientist interested in cardiovascular dynamics with whom to study. Further, as always, we needed to pay attention to the incessant demands of the case—to reach organizations such as the National Student Association, the American Association of University Professors, the ACLU, the Emergency Civil Liberties Committee, the American Friends Service Committee, and others that could buttress our legal arguments with amicus briefs addressed to the Supreme Court.

And, of course, all day, every day, our children needed and deserved our attention.

JEAN

We were heartened when the American Civil Liberties Union, in July 1961, strongly urged the NSF to reinstate Ed's fellowship and repeal the National Defense Education Act affidavit. Then, in December, under the title, "Crimes and Science Fellowships," *Science* published a strong letter signed by six prominent scientists, including Nobel Laureate S. E. Luria of M.I.T., addressing the newly revised NSF application forms, which required students to list crimes of which they had been convicted: "Crimes involving intellectual dishonesty" these scientists wrote, "would be of grave concern to a university. On the other hand, certain actions that are crimes in the eyes of the law have little relation to the fitness of a person to contribute to scientific knowledge, and thereby to serve the country and the world. For instance, an applicant might have been imprisoned for taking part in a demonstration against segregation in a Southern state, or for being a conscientious objector. Or he might have refused, on the basis of the First Amendment, to give certain testimony before a Congressional committee. Such crimes may be evidence not of a defect of character but of exceptionally uncompromising independence and integrity. . . . We can hardly assume that a government agency, under the watchful eye of Congress, would feel free to support a politically cantankerous but brilliant applicant. Indeed, one cannot escape the suspicion that the bill is aimed precisely at such persons. The bill thus appears to represent, in veiled form, a return to an earlier McCarthyite obsession with internal security. . . . The danger from a rare fellowship award to a person of questionable character is small; the long-term danger from creating an atmosphere of intellectual intimidation is large."

On December 28, *Science* reported that "one quick result" of the repeal of the non-Communist affidavit under the NDEA was the inclusion of seventeen colleges and universities that had been abstaining from the loan program because of the affidavit. The repeal, it explained, "has quieted controversy in which issues of academic freedom and civil rights were raised."

In the March 2, 1962 issue of *Science*, the six scientists modified their position. They did not, they explained, oppose the entire revised NSF bill, which they judged as a whole "beneficial, since it repeals the present ineffective requirement that each applicant submit a sworn affidavit concerning his political beliefs. . . . Our objection is specifically to the section of this bill requiring applicants for a fellowship from the NSF to list previous criminal convictions or pending charges."

That was the end of it. Ed's strongest scientific supporters had concluded that it was permissible for the government to ask about an applicant's criminal history, seeing this as preferable to requiring him or her to sign additional loyalty oaths. The White House congratulated the NSF for having avoided a major publicity flap over Ed's fellowship; the NSF congratulated itself for having soothed the congressional committees by revoking Ed's fellowship and for moving forward from McCarthyism by recommending the stronger strictures for NSF applicants favored by HUAC and the Science and Astronautics Committee. In a final congressional compromise, even the affidavits that had been routinely required of students applying for NDEA loans and NSF fellowships were abolished.

Ed? He was out of luck.

ED

So there we were in 1961: The NSF had revoked my fellowship for '61–'64, and my two-year Ford Foundation traineeship ($3,800 per year) was due to end. Our attorneys were working pro bono. We wanted to stay at Illinois, but with three kids who needed to eat every day, we had to consider leaving.

I had finished my coursework and was ready to take my preliminaries and write a thesis proposal. All fellowships and traineeships for the year had already been awarded, and we were desperate for income. I drew up a family budget for the 1962–'63 academic year—$5,670.

The dean of engineering told me that the university president said that there was no reason that I was not eligible to receive university support, but that unfortunately there were no longer any research funds available for the next academic year. My request for a tuition and fee waiver was denied for lack of funds.

One letter from a student suggested that I contact Professor William Davidon, a noted antiwar activist and nuclear physicist from Haverford College. When I did, he referred me to the Society for Social Responsibility in Science, in whose newsletter I placed an ad (the fee was waived due to my limited finances) seeking a position as a research assistant in a lab where I could, hopefully, pursue my interests in hemodynamics, the study of blood flow. Unfortunately, I received no offers. Several other contacts also proved fruitless.

JEAN

The bottom drawer of our old rolltop desk still contains the 3"x5" card catalog I sporadically kept from 1958 until 1963 in a serious effort to build and maintain a defense committee. With the desk, the cards have moved with us across the country several times. Created long before the computer, the catalog consists of hundreds

of cards, each headed with the name of someone we thought might help. Today, I am amazed that so many people sent money, usually very small amounts ($2 or $5), and that a few sent those amounts repeatedly.

On October 9, 1961, the United States Supreme Court granted certiorari; our case would be argued that season and a decision could be expected in June. The Court's decision to hear the case was heralded by the *St. Louis Post-Dispatch* in an editorial entitled "Between Two Decisions." It explained that, relying on the 1957 *Watkins* decision in which the Court had ruled that HUAC "had exceeded its authority and that there was no power of exposure for the sake of exposure," Ed had cited his First Amendment right to refuse to answer HUAC's questions. He was not indicted for another year, however—after the Court's 1959 ruling in *Barenblatt* that the committee's authority was "unassailable." Arguing that the earlier opinion "encouraged Mr. Yellin to take a position which [the] second opinion largely destroyed," and that his appeal "raises grave questions about the Un-American Committee's precise authority and power of exposure," the editorial urged that the Court clarify its thinking.

Aware of our financial situation, Professor Seichi Konzo, bless his heart, arranged a $3,600 Ford Foundation loan. Internal correspondence from the Ford Foundation Archives (Henry T. Heald to Harvey B. Matthews) shows that during the NSF disaster, when the press had characterized Ed as a Ford Fellow, the foundation had made "calls . . . to the Washington desks of the wire services and the principal American newspapers. . . . The next day they left out any references to the Foundation." Now Professor Konzo wrote to members of the Ford Foundation in Illinois and to the Foundation's science and engineering director in New York, reminding them that they had authorized a $1,600 loan for the 1961–'62 academic year and that a fellowship and loan had been tentatively authorized for 1962–'63.

As we believed, the FBI was keeping a careful tally of our money. A file headed "Source of Funds" describes "records of the business office, University of Illinois, show[ing] that sizeable disbursements have been made to subject [Ed] from the Ford Foundation Faculty Development Fund as follows: June 1, 1961, suspect was authorized to receive a total of $1,600. He received $900 on this date and the balance of $700 on December 1, 1961. On January 1, 1962, he was authorized to receive an additional $2,800. He received $1,000 on January 1, 1962, and the balance of $180 on March 2, 1963."

On January 2, 1962, Ed received a note from the Reverend David Cole, minister of the Unitarian Universalist church in Urbana. It was accompanied by a check for $500, to be repaid without interest on January 1, 1967. The lenders were not named.

ED

We were, of course, most thankful. In our situation, $500 was a huge amount. We reasoned that it must have come from a faculty member who wished to remain anonymous. Six years later, David Cole sent me a note from his new home in Maryland, writing that he still had the file on the old financial matter, and that if were interested, he would contact that "other party."

In 1970, two years after I had been on the faculty of the Albert Einstein College of Medicine for five years, I finally felt secure enough to send David a check for $100. He replied that he would try to locate the two donors. "It was not easy to track them down. They are pleased that you are in a position to effect repayment."

Within the week, I received a handwritten note from Woody Anderson, who, like me, had been a graduate student and a Ford Foundation fellow. "Absolutely delighted to hear you're in a position with a bit of security and confidence. We're really pleased to have been of some help when needed."

CHAPTER EIGHT

Under the Velvet Glove

ED

Professor Sam Talbot reassured me, when I told him all the details of my political past, that "Johns Hopkins University stood by Owen Lattimore and we will stand by you!" Lattimore was a Johns Hopkins distinguished professor whom Senator McCarthy had labeled "the top Soviet espionage agent in the United States." Professor Talbot's announcement gave me hope.

My first contact with Sam Talbot had been in July 1961, when I learned that he was the principal investigator of a biomedical engineering program at the Johns Hopkins University Medical School. I reached out to him for two important reasons: Having lost my NSF Fellowship, I was desperate for a source of funding while working on my thesis, and I needed to be at an institution, or in a program, that could provide guidance in bioengineering, a relatively new field of study. I thought that it had the potential to be more useful to humanity than mechanical engineering, which, during the height of the Cold War in the '60s, was focused on military applications. The Illinois faculty was strong in rocket science, requiring the study of very high-velocity gases. In contrast, my interest in blood flow required a knowledge of relatively low-velocity liquid flow. Also, let's face it, my political background made it highly unlikely for me to find a stimulating job in classical engineering.

I had already decided on the fluid mechanics of arterial blood flow as a thesis research area. I needed both funding for the project and a suitable research environment. I scoured the medical journals looking for predoctoral training programs. I looked through the biophysics literature and at bioengineering reports for contacts who might be interested in my research. I searched for sympathetic sources who might inform me of leads, but the responses were either "no" or "not until the Supreme Court hands down a decision." Finally, I found Professor Talbot's program listed in a medical journal, with a call for applicants to start in the following year.

Professor Talbot held appointments at Johns Hopkins in both medicine and bioengineering at a time when bioengineering was a young and growing discipline seeking to apply physical and mathematical methods and principles to research in biological systems. I was fortunate to have learned that Talbot had recently become the principal investigator within a unique National Institutes of Health program designed to provide predoctoral training in bioengineering. Typically, such a program would aim to graduate an entering student in at least five, but more likely six or seven, years. Since I was already well on the way to finishing my coursework, deciding on a thesis project, and taking my prelims, I was in a favorable position, possibly able to complete my PhD in three years. It is common knowledge in the research community that funding agencies and review committees look at both the quality and the quantity of results when they examine the progress of grants. My participation in the training program could demonstrate rapid progress.

Professor Talbot considered my background and made me the following offer: I was to arrange with the mechanical engineering department at Illinois to do my research as a special student at Hopkins, while remaining a student in absentia at Illinois. Talbot's offer was a tremendous opportunity for many obvious reasons. In particular, it carried a stipend of $300 per month for three years— enough time for me to complete my thesis research. Supplemented by Jean's tiny part-time salary for teaching freshman rhetoric, and by loans from the Ford Foundation, it would be enough income for us. Professor Talbot and I met in February 1962 at the annual meeting of the Biophysics Society in Washington, D.C. A month later I was admitted to Hopkins as a student in engineering, and in April, I was awarded a fellowship in the bioengineering program.

I felt exceptionally warm toward Professor Talbot not only because he successfully placed me in his important program, but also because before the Supreme Court heard my case, he committed himself to helping me. In essence, he made a commitment to me knowing I might end up in jail while under his mentorship. Too many other "sympathetic" correspondents had deferred considering help until after the Supreme Court decision, which was due in June. (Another exception was Professor Alan Burton, a distinguished biophysicist at the University of Western Ontario, who expressed interest in my research, was impressed with my record at the University of Illinois, and was not concerned about my political past. He went so far as to sponsor me for a fellowship at the Canadian National Research Council, which approved my application, but the Canadian government would not approve it while I was under the "supervision" of the American judicial system.)

JEAN

Relieved and delighted as I was that Ed had miraculously managed to move forward, get to Hopkins, and find a way to complete his PhD despite HUAC's determination to destroy his chance for a scientific career, I was afraid. I, too, had a degree to earn, and I had no confidence whatever that I would be able to complete my coursework in American literature and write my dissertation at Johns Hopkins. I needed to meet with my major professor, who holed up in a carrel on the fourth floor of the library, so up, up, up the stairs I went.

Professor Sherman Paul was extremely supportive, which was a terrific relief, as only months earlier he had reduced me to tears when I had asked him to serve as my thesis advisor. Although agreeing, he had announced that he planned to accept no more female doctoral students because he needed to husband his energy and expend it on students who would not be too emotional and, without family distractions, would devote themselves to their work. A Harvard PhD, he now assured me that my work would be adequate for the Ivy League. Such a relief!

ED

Throwing out a broad net had produced another very important contact for me. I had been searching the literature for problems in fluid dynamics that could be used as my thesis project. Fortunately, a small number of biophysicists were interested in the relation between blood flow and turbulence in the arterial system.

A liquid, like blood, that is flowing in a tube will be either orderly, flowing in an undisturbed state, or disorderly, flowing in a disturbed state. The former is called laminar, the latter turbulent. As in most physical states, orderly conditions consume less energy than disorderly ones. Turbulence in blood flow thus consumes more energy, that is, requires more work by the heart, than laminar flow. There was also evidence that turbulence in the flowing blood might injure red blood cells and the walls of arteries. Much was known about the conditions that led laminar flow in a tube to become turbulent under conditions of steady flow, but arterial blood flow is pulsatile, that is, it rises and falls with each heartbeat, and nothing was known about the transition from laminar to turbulent flow under pulsatile conditions. It was a no-brainer! For my thesis research, I would propose studying the conditions under which a liquid transitions from laminar to turbulent flow when the driving force is time-variant, that is, when it is simulating a heartlike pump.

A Swedish researcher named Lars Lindgren had developed a technique to study turbulence in tubes using a novel method of streaming birefringence (an optical property of a material). He had published several papers investigating the characteristics of turbulence in a fluid flowing at a steady state, that is, at a velocity that did not vary with time; his experiments were designed to produce many different velocities, but each one did not vary with time. In my thesis, I used the same experimental setup, but I designed a pumping system that produced a flow with a pulsatile velocity, that is, a velocity that varied with time, and modeled the flow of blood pumped from a beating heart into the aorta.

By a great stroke of luck, Lindgren wrote that he would be soon be in residence at Johns Hopkins University in the department of applied mechanics, a world-recognized center of excellence, and would be happy to mentor me if I came to Hopkins. Professor Talbot agreed that this would be a great opportunity for me.

Upon my return to Illinois, I discussed the offer with Professors Konzo and Korst, both of whom agreed with the proposed arrangement, and why not? It would relieve the University of Illinois of responsibility for me and get me off campus. I would no longer be an object of controversy. I was given permission to complete my dissertation in absentia, to have my research supervised by Lindgren and other highly respected faculty members, and then to defend my thesis at the University of Illinois. This relieved the university from having to deny me financial support, at least until the Supreme Court ruled, and also relieved the mechanical engineering department from having to find research support for me.

Professor Talbot worked out the details of my becoming a special student, and all we now needed was to find a position at Hopkins that would tide me over until my fellowship began in September. Professor Talbot once again demonstrated his concern for my family's well-being and for my political and legal condition by wisely advising me to find a position at Hopkins that would not involve government funding. "It probably would be better to have an employment status," he wrote, "where the eager beavers from Washington would not have access to the names of employees."

Thus began a new period in our saga. In July, we arranged for the children to stay with friends in Champaign-Urbana while Jean and I drove to Baltimore to find a place to live for the anticipated three years it would take to complete my thesis research. Fortunately, Shike and Lola Gellman, old friends from the Coops—the Amalgamated Housing Project in the Bronx where I grew up—who were living in Baltimore at the time, helped us find a nice small row house for rent in a pleasant neighborhood. We signed a year's lease and arrived on August 15, 1962, in time to meet the mover, unpack, and enroll Peter, Lisa, and Michael in school.

JEAN

I cannot remember the house-hunting drive to Baltimore with Ed, nor signing the lease on a house near a school in the Pimlico district, nor rushing back to Urbana and the kids. I vaguely remember packing, stacking our books in boxes from the liquor store (they were strongest). I cannot remember calling a mover, nor the move itself, nor locating the kids' school and teaching them how to walk there and home. But I do remember our house: two stories with a staircase on the right in the front hall, with a telephone next to the stairs. That phone was Ed's connection to Hopkins, and my connection to Ed.

ED

Within days, I phoned Professor Talbot to set up a meeting with Lindgren and the applied mechanics faculty members—and was told to come to campus as soon as possible. Something was not right!

Johns Hopkins University had been informed (I wasn't told by whom) that it would not be permitted to use government funds to support me or my research. A world-renowned professor of applied mechanics at a world-renowned institution told me: "If the government finds out that you have used anything purchased with government funds, even a pencil, Johns Hopkins will lose all government support!"

This was how frightened some people were under McCarthyism! (I do not believe that Hopkins was actually told this, although I know from my FBI files that the university was told I could not receive the fellowship that Talbot had provided, nor use equipment purchased by government funds.)

In contrast to all of the publicity when the National Science

Foundation had revoked my fellowship, this was done quietly, without any public discussion. The FBI had learned that I had been awarded a fellowship funded by the National Institutes of Health, and they acted quickly to get the word to Hopkins that I should not be eligible to receive government funds. On August 22, 1962, J. Edgar Hoover himself arranged for his subordinates to brief Secretary of Health Education and Welfare Anthony Celebrezze that I was "a Security Index subject and should not be eligible to receive government funds." I had been blacklisted by the United States government.

But all was not lost. As frightened as Hopkins was, and as appalled as I was, we did discuss alternatives to government support so that I could stay at Hopkins and work with Lindgren on my thesis. The applied mechanics department was willing to provide space if I could raise the money for equipment and machine-shop time. I estimated that approximately $8,000 would be required for equipment, and another $300 per month for living expenses, which the fellowship would have provided.

I turned to a sympathetic contact with whom I had discussed my situation by mail since September 1961: John H. Peters, associate medical director for research at the American Heart Association. He proved to be a source of important information as well as a source of moral support. I had met Dr. Peters in New York City in the summer of 1961, when I gave him our "fact sheet" providing a detailed chronology and description of the "Yellin Case." He was sympathetic to my plight, although he did not necessarily support my politics. His contribution consisted of providing me with the names of some prominent scientists who might be interested in my research plans. Sadly, with one exception, the responses to my pleas were of little value. One prominent scientist, however, did respond with a wonderfully sympathetic and understanding letter, but it concluded with "my present interests do not coincide with yours." Dr. Peters advised me to apply for an emergency grant from the American Heart Association to cover the $8,000 cost of my proposed research. When I expressed some skepticism regarding Johns Hopkins' willingness to support my grant application, he responded, "You are too used to dealing with universities like

Illinois, but at Harvard and Hopkins, things will be different." I grew hopeful.

Professor Talbot agreed to apply on our behalf to the American Heart Association. Vic Rabinowitz contacted Gerard Piel, his Harvard classmate who was the publisher of *Scientific American*. He suggested that I contact Horace Davis, treasurer of the Marion Davis Scholarship Fund, established in the name of a teacher and activist who was an advocate for racial justice and the rights of labor, to provide "support to students working for peace and justice." Accordingly, I applied and received a small scholarship for the academic year 1962.

But the gods were against me. I had been admitted to Hopkins as a "special student" because I was still enrolled at the University of Illinois, albeit in absentia, and when I met with the Hopkins administration to go over the process of applying for the grant, I was informed that the school had a policy of not supporting grants for "special students." Without support, I could not do my thesis research. What was to be done?

Someone, I don't remember who, suggested the obvious: an appeal to the American Association of University Professors. Of course, the AAUP. We wrote to the national office in Washington and were referred to the president of the Hopkins chapter, Carl Christ, a professor of political economy.

Decades later, while I was doing research for this book and in answer to my queries, Johns Hopkins would inform me that there were no records of my experiences there, including my involvement with Dr. Milton Eisenhower, President Dwight D. Eisenhower's brother, who was then the president of Johns Hopkins University. (Although he was not a medical doctor, and did not have a PhD, Eisenhower was referred to as Dr.) When I wrote again citing relevant dates, I was again told that there were no records, and that Dr. Eisenhower had left few papers. However, because of Carl Christ's commitment to academic freedom—and his meticulous note-taking—I am able to provide a complete and accurate narrative of the events at Hopkins. Working from my scattered papers and Professor Christ's careful notes, I can report that on September 10, 1962, I met him in his office and he listened to my story.

The next day, after conferring with Professor Talbot and an AAUP colleague, he made an appointment to discuss the situation with Dr. Eisenhower. On September 12, he met with Dr. Eisenhower and colleagues to discuss the problem. After seeing Johns Hopkins' two letters to me—the second of which unconditionally offered tuition plus $300 a month for ten months—all agreed that I was entitled to regard this as a commitment. The belief was expressed that external pressure should not govern the university's decisions about teaching and research, but, ironically, no decision was reached concerning my situation.

The next morning, Dr. Eisenhower arranged for a meeting with Professor Christ and indicated that he had discussed the matter with the university's legal counsel, who suggested three possible courses of action. That afternoon, he asked various members of the bioengineering faculty to meet with him, and he invited me to join them. There was general agreement that deferring admission would not be justified, and we discussed alternatives to government support so that I could stay at Hopkins and work with Lindgren.

The next day, Dr. Eisenhower asked various faculty and officials to meet with him before presenting the university's decision to me. When he and I met, the decision he proposed was that Hopkins would not revoke my admission as a special student. If I agreed to stay, the university would provide tuition and $300 a month for ten months from nonfederal funds—with the understanding that if I should have to begin a prison term, the payments would be stopped, to resume upon my return. I would not be permitted to use facilities financed by federal funds, but laboratory space would be made available by the applied mechanics department, if I could raise the money for equipment and machine-shop time. The university would adhere to its policy of declining to sign its corporate name to any application for funds on behalf of a special student. If, however, funds should be offered to Hopkins for the purpose of supporting my research, the university would accept and administer the gift. Alternatively, should I decide instead to do my research at the University of Illinois, Hopkins would pay me $3,000 in a lump sum from nonfederal funds.

I was invited to discuss Dr. Eisenhower's decision with appropriate faculty and with my family. I knew that I had the support of the faculty, particularly the willingness of Professor Lindgren to be my mentor, and recognized the superiority of the Hopkins faculty compared to the Illinois faculty in the area of my interest. On the other hand, I realized that my thesis research would take at least two, possibly three years, and Hopkins was committed to only one year of support. It was not likely that the FBI would forget me, or that the government would change its evil ways and forget about my refusal to answer HUAC's questions. The FBI knew that I had given up my connection to the Communist Party, but as long as I refused to submit to HUAC's interrogation, I was kept on their "security list." I was also aware that my status as a "special student" made my position at Hopkins subject to unforeseen circumstances.

I therefore told Dr. Eisenhower that I would return to Illinois. I tried to take the high ground and agreed that instead of $3,000 in a lump sum, I should receive $300 a month for ten months, with an interruption were I to spend time in prison, and with a resumption should I return to full-time study afterwards, just as if I were to receive it at Hopkins.

JEAN

It was a rocky week. What I remember best was singing along with Pete Seeger's new record, which seemed prescient: "To everything there is a season, turn, turn, turn . . . a time to win, a time to lose; a time to be born, a time to die." Ecclesiastes felt uniquely appropriate.

Our children hated Baltimore. They told me they didn't want to line up to enter the school; in class, they didn't want to pray or salute the flag. Lisa remembers having to walk to school and back by herself, which she hadn't done before, and once getting lost. Peter remembers a big hill on which he flipped over his bike handlebars, and once being five cents short on his school lunch money. "The teacher fronted me that five cents," he told me, "and I never paid her back." Michael remembers seeing pushcarts full of candies and cheap toys just outside the school fence, where kids would buy things before entering the school gate. "I remember candy lips and mustaches and all sorts of goodies I had never seen before," Michael recalls. "And in class I remember prayer being part of our morning routine. I really had no clue what this was all about, but prayer in school was a real thing then."

After it became obvious that Ed could not stay at Hopkins, we phoned Urbana friends to arrange for the housing office to find us a unit in Stadium Terrace, and I phoned the English Department to ask for two sections of Freshman Rhetoric to teach. And so we packed up the car and drove back, and I began teaching the next morning.

That weekend, we were welcomed home with a big party. Our across-the-road neighbors baked a large sheet cake decorated with chocolate frosting and "O SHIT" written in white icing. Delicious. Our lives were back to familiar rhythms and my routine went back to normal: lunches to pack, a school bus to catch, classes to meet, papers to grade. What was unusual was that for the next twelve months, the mailman monthly delivered a plain manila envelope that inside held a Johns Hopkins University envelope containing, as promised, Ed's monthly stipend.

ED

Before leaving Baltimore, I met with Professor Talbot, gave him a fond farewell, and reminded him of our first meeting, when he had reassured me, "We stood by Owen Lattimore, and we'll stand by you." I will never forget his response, "Under the velvet glove is a mailed fist!"

CHAPTER NINE

Not Fine for Yellin

JEAN

Viewing it from the twenty-first century, we are amazed that Ed's first U.S. Supreme Court hearing did not seem memorable. Ed and I loaned our kids to Aaron and Louise, then flew to Washington, where Vic argued our case against a nondescript government attorney whom we do not remember at all, except that we were not impressed by his arguments or presentation. Only eight justices were sitting: Felix Frankfurter, who was ill, did not hear the argument. As I recall, Vic's presentation was impressive, but it was not easy to follow his arguments, which seemed thorough and detailed. The government presented a forty-five-page brief that included a twenty-four-page argument. Victor presented a thirty-five-page brief that included a twenty-three-page argument. The ACLU presented a short amicus brief on Ed's behalf, arguing that *Barenblatt*, *Wilkinson*, and *Braden* should all be overruled and Ed's conviction reversed. Then Ed and I flew home to our children and waited for a decision. And waited. And waited. The wait seemed endless.

In June, instead of reaching a decision, the Court ordered reargument. We assumed that this was because the Court was split 4–4—which would have meant that the ruling of the lower court would hold, and Ed would go to jail. Instead, somehow Chief Justice Earl Warren (who had, amazingly, caused the *Brown v. Board of Education of Topeka* school desegregation decision to be unanimous) had convinced his colleagues to rehear Ed's case before a full court. Then Frankfurter retired, and President John F. Kennedy appointed Arthur Goldberg, who joined the Court in September 1962.

In the meantime, Ed's case was scheduled to be reheard again on December 6, 1962.

This time, we decided to take Peter, who was almost eleven, to Washington with us. It was many years later that we learned that when we had left home to return to the Supreme Court, seven-year-old Michael had kissed his father good-bye, thinking that Ed was leaving forever. When Michael confided in his big sister, eight-year-old Lisa, she had reassured him: "Don't be stupid! They wouldn't have taken Peter with them if it wasn't all right."

PETER

I was the oldest kid, I was almost eleven, and I understood what was going on. I remember that we flew into National Airport in a twin-engine turbo-prop plane. We came in right over the water. And I remember we went into the Supreme Court and there were lots of steps up into the building, and it was very big and mono-lithic and authoritative, like nothing they have in Champaign, Illinois. The closest thing to it would be the football stadium.

The Supreme Court had a hugely high ceiling. They handed us a card that had the justices' names and the order they sit in up on the bench. They were very high up, looking down at piles of books next to them, with pages bringing them more and more books. They kept conferring as if they were not paying attention to what was really going on, not to the arguments.

We couldn't sit and read anything, couldn't have a newspaper or a book. We had to be sitting facing the justices, watching the proceedings and waiting for them to call my Dad's case.

We broke for lunch and went downstairs to a cafeteria under-neath the Supreme Court building. When we went back upstairs, the case was already being argued.

JEAN

It was at this proceeding that the controversy over HUAC and the First Amendment was most clearly voiced. Signaling the significance of the issues involved, U.S. Solicitor General Archibald Cox himself argued for the government. (Cox would later win fame when, serving as special prosecutor, he demanded the Watergate tapes, prompting President Nixon to order his attorney general and then his deputy attorney general to dismiss him. When both refused and resigned, Acting Attorney General Robert Bork finally fired Cox.)

For the government, Cox presented a ninety-one-page brief augmented by a six-page appendix. It asserted that HUAC's use of compulsory process to obtain Ed's testimony was a valid exercise of congressional power; that the trial court properly excluded Professor Emerson's testimony; that the House resolution authorizing HUAC was not constitutionally vague; that HUAC rules did not require that Ed's request to appear at an executive session be granted; and that the questions about Communist colonization in the Gary steel unions were not too vague.

Ed was so impressed by the skilled presentation of the crew-cutted, bow-tied, preppy Cox that he joked, "You're right! Take me away!"

ED

Jean was not impressed by my sense of humor.

JEAN

Not me. I found Victor's reargument compelling. He began by agreeing with Cox: "This controversy involves Constitutional issues of such magnitude that the Court must never rest in its examination of them, even in the case of prior decisions." He then argued that at issue was not (as the government asserted) the relationship

between the Court and the Congress, but between the Congress
and the citizens, and "the extent to which the former may control
the political activities of the latter."

He stated that "for over two decades, the Committee [HUAC]
has been a major repressive force against the exercise of activities
supposed to be protected by the First Amendment . . . it has stifled
the dialogue that has characterized a free society, 'so that even in
these days, no debate takes place on crucial issues.'" (The quoted
phrase came from Justice William O. Douglas's essay, "The Sub-
merged American," in *Frontier Magazine*, August 1962. Sister Ann
and Victor had collaborated to use several quotations directly from
the justices' own writings in our brief.)

The Gary hearings, Vic argued, were "one of hundreds which
the Committee has conducted under the vague provisions of its
charter, which gave it jurisdiction over Un-American propaganda."
Ed Yellin "is not an isolated unwilling witness; the overwhelming
majority of the witnesses called by the Committee has refused to
answer questions. His case is not the exception—it is the rule. . . .
Our democratic society, together with the Yellins . . . is a co-
petitioner in these cases."

Bolstered with an amicus brief by Osmund Frankel of the American Civil Liberties Union, Vic voiced fundamental objections to
the concept of balancing the needs of the government for testimony against the individual rights of witnesses, as the Court had
done in *Barenblatt*. "The task of balancing, or even comparing
rights and interests such as these, is for the metaphysician, not
the lawyer." He then argued that even with such a balancing test,
however, Ed's constitutional interest should weigh more heavily:
"How many times must we have this same testimony before it is
weighed as a grain of sand against the mighty rights of the individual? Is there never a time when more inquiries weigh very little
against the right of petitioner and the right of a free society to
enjoy without governmental interference the privileges granted by
the First Amendment?"

If we were to balance these claims, he continued, Professor
Emerson's testimony should have been admitted because it chal-
lenged "facts" that the Court had accepted without argument in

Barenblatt, Braden, and *Wilkinson*—namely, that the American Communist Party presented an imminent threat to the U.S. government. If the Court persisted in attempting to balance the government's need for testimony and citizens' rights, he predicted, cases would come before the Court concerning burden of proof and admissibility of evidence not only concerning "subversive" activity, but relating to the struggle of the Negro people in the South for equal rights.

Arguing that the statute under which Ed was convicted was unconstitutionally vague, Vic noted that it had only been a few months since Chief Justice Warren had asked, "Who can define the words 'un-American?'" Concerning Ed's right to be heard at an executive session, he quoted from Rep. Walter's testimony at Ed's trial: "I am sure that had you communicated this whole matter to the committee before we left Washington so that we could have given it due consideration—we would have, and always do—we might have a different situation today." Vic concluded that Ed's conviction should be reversed and his indictment dismissed.

PETER

The justices didn't seem to be paying a whole lot of attention to the argument that was going on, and they would interrupt and ask questions. That wasn't the way I thought courtroom proceedings were supposed to be conducted. But, of course, that's the Supreme Court. I remember it seemed that they were done listening before the lawyers were done presenting. They had heard enough, and just stopped. Then they went on to the next case, I presume, and we left.

I remember not having a feeling of closure, that we left and it was going to take five or six months before we even knew how long it would take. Why couldn't they make a decision tonight at dinner? I mean, what more were they going to learn that would take them five or six months? That seemed like a long time to make up your mind about something, especially about somebody's father.

JEAN

Today, Lisa recalls those days as intense—and that she couldn't figure out what was causing the stress. Money? Her parents being in school? Her mom being behind on her dissertation or having too many papers to grade? It wasn't until she was much older that she understood that all of that stress and confusion was based on her father's case, and was not typical of family life.

As for me, I could not imagine what I would do were Ed to go to jail. Nor could our friends, who later told us that for years they had debated our future. We did manage to keep the children somewhat secure by remaining in Urbana. As for the future, we chose not to think about it.

Between the second court hearing in December and the promised date of decision in June, the wait seemed endless.

ED

Writing the court's decision, Chief Justice Earl Warren, speaking for the majority, acknowledged my challenge: "Since the case presented Constitutional questions of continued importance, we granted *certiorari*" (judicial review). But he then refused to address those questions: "However, because the view we take of the Committee's action, which was at variance with its rules, we do not reach the Constitutional questions raised. The Constitutional questions upon which we need not pass are whether the Committee's investigation infringed upon petitioner's rights under the First Amendment and whether petitioner was convicted under an unconstitutionally vague statute. In addition, we do not discuss petitioner's contention that the trial judge erred in excluding expert testimony about the factors which should be considered in determining petitioner's rights under the First Amendment."

Quoting from the Gary hearings and my trial, Warren only addressed, for fourteen pages, the fourth and least significant point that Vic had raised: that HUAC had violated its own rules by failing to consider my request for an executive session.

His 5–4 majority opinion was followed by a dissent by Justice Byron White, joined by Justices John Marshall Harlan, Tom Clark, and Potter Stewart, who for twenty-six pages examined the Gary hearings and my trial and ruled that HUAC had not failed to apply its executive session rule to me. Their dissent concluded that "oversight of congressional committee procedures [by the Court] should not be based upon such frivolous grounds."

JEAN

Recounting all of this in his memoir, *Unrepentant Leftist*, Vic wrote: "This was fine for Yellin, who was home free, but a disappointment to me and of no significance at all in the struggle for First Amendment rights. The Constitutional issues that were not decided were much more interesting and important than the trivial issues on which the court spent so much time and energy."

ED

Actually, it was not fine for Yellin. Vic was wrong. I hadn't endured those five years just to stay out of prison. I had hoped that my action would strengthen the struggle to uphold the First Amendment rights of the American people. I had hoped that it would slow and eventually halt the witch hunts that plagued the country during McCarthyism. I hadn't chosen to be called before HUAC, but once called I could not, in good conscience, do anything but assert my constitutional rights of free speech and association. I would not be a party to HUAC's assault on our freedoms.

But make no mistake: it was an enormous burden on the Yellin family from the beginning. Think of how I felt on reading the cover of the trial record: *United States of America v. Edward Yellin*. That's 179 million against one.

JEAN

How to write about our victory? Peter probably did it best.

PETER

I remember taking the call about winning the case. I remember Dad picking up the phone and looking . . . different, his head tilted, his face full of feeling. "Okay, we won" was the first thing out of his mouth. It was almost comical. I remember it had to be serious yet it wasn't a serious moment. It was a moment of joy. There was all this elation: We had won the case. All the potluck dinner people, the Unitarians and the Quakers, and the people at the university, it was like: WHEE!

And I remember the party—to which the folks didn't invite us. They made us go to bed at 8:00. Tap the keg and everybody came over to the house and made a huge amount of noise, and we were supposed to be going to sleep. There were three of us in the room, and there were maybe a hundred outside the door.

JEAN

It was thoughtless that we didn't invite our children to join us, but in victory, as throughout the ordeal, we worked hard not to let "the case" take over our lives.

There was a huge banner that stretched across the road. It read, "YELLIN SI!! HUAC NO!" I saved that banner—we still have it.

ED

There was quite another party in New York. First came an event organized by the New York Council to Abolish HUAC at Town Hall in Manhattan. I spoke there to a medium-sized crowd about "a total lack of respect for the individual, aside from the infringement of First Amendment rights." I commented on inaccuracies in the press, noting that a reporter had written that I had two children, "prompting the boys to ask why their sister was left out." It was reporters, I said, who had informed me of my contempt citation and who later told me of court decisions.

Members of the board of the National Science Foundation had spent an entire day discussing my case without giving me a chance to appear. My conclusion: The persecution of one individual is significant, but need not be overwhelming. "Strength can be found in many forms from many sources."

JEAN

The party that followed the Town Hall meeting was overwhelming for me, not because of the people or the conversation, but because of the setting: a penthouse apartment with a lovely roof garden amid the bright city lights and under the stars. I had never been in such a place before, but soon enough we retrieved our children from their grandparents in nearby Goldens Bridge and we all drove home to Urbana, where we resumed our lives.

In the end, nothing happened to all eleven of the Gary men who, citing their First Amendment rights, refused to answer HUAC's questions and were threatened with contempt of Congress. None lost his job, and of the four men indicted, only Ed went to trial. Throughout the five years that his case was in the courts, however, the other three men charged with contempt lived in a difficult state of suspended animation.

Bob Lehrer, a Colorado teacher who found himself on the front page of the *Rocky Mountain News*, was warned by his superintendent that he would be fired. Bob sought help among the Quakers, who introduced him to a lawyer who chaired the ACLU, and went with him to the superintendent. The superintendent backed off, and Bob was rehired by his principal the following year.

Vic Malis found the stress of waiting under indictment to be very painful.

Al Samter continued living as before, remaining involved in the steelworkers union until he retired, then sparking an activist group of former steelworkers.

After the Gary hearings, no subsequent group of HUAC witnesses followed their lead by invoking First Amendment rights as the basis of their refusal to respond to their interrogators. The Gary men did not, as we had hoped, become a model for others to follow. HUAC continued their red-hunting junkets, although they were increasingly denounced.

Back in 1960 in San Francisco, asserting that they were quelling a riot, police attacked students who tried to enter crowded HUAC hearings. The protestors were doused with fire hoses and dragged down the marble steps beneath the rotunda at City Hall. In a film, *Operation Abolition*, HUAC members condemned the "student rioters," and in response the Northern California Civil Liberties Union produced *Operation Correction*, a 1960 motion picture exposing HUAC's inaccuracies. (Scenes from both the hearings and the protest were included in Mark Kitchell's 1990 documentary, *Berkeley in the Sixties,* which was nominated for a documentary Academy Award.)

In 1967—in contrast to the Gary steelworkers who had worn suits saved for weddings and funerals and had cited the Constitution to challenge HUAC—wildly garbed Yippies costumed like Uncle Sam and Santa Claus defied HUAC. Two years later, it changed its name to the House Committee on Internal Security. It finally died in 1975.

So we had not stopped the machine. But it hadn't stopped us, either.

What did we learn from our struggle with HUAC? We learned that it isn't much fun to be the friction that slows the machine. You don't even know if it is you who has slowed it—or if, with so many mini-mechanisms, the machine has really slowed. Still, stopping the machine is the essential goal and must come first, fun or no fun at all. Much better to proceed, or to attempt to proceed, as if your task were simply to plant some seeds that perhaps will flourish among its rusting parts.

The HUAC hearing and its aftermath transformed all five members of our family, not only during the years we spent fighting "the case," but still today. Recently I was asked, Did *U.S. vs. Yellin* make a professional difference for Ed or for me? We can't really know the answer to that question, but after achieving his PhD, Ed went to the University of Washington for a post-doc, then lived out a satisfying thirty-five-year career at Albert Einstein College of Medicine in the Bronx, pursuing his research in bioengineering and teaching physiology to medical students. As for me, professionally, the question has never even come up.

In the 1950s Chan Davis wrote in *The Purge* that "universities, in order to maintain a level of intellectual challenge they require for health, ought to display to potential dissenters a moderate welcome to dissent," and that a minimum in this direction would be "ostentatiously restoring the radicals who had been expelled."

Victor Rabinowitz's argument before the court encompassed not only the academy but all of American discourse. He argued that the health of our democracy demands that not only majority viewpoints are essential, but that all points of view are necessary; that when HUAC and other repressive entities systematically attempt to stop leftist ideas from being expressed, the national discourse is impoverished. Surely it looked that way in the 1950s. But then came the '60s, with all sorts of voices and ideas unleashed. And today, various folks are running for political office embracing the once-forbidden word, SOCIALISM.

The Earth does move.

AFTERWORD

In Contempt is a story American leftists need to read now, as we consider what we need most to reweave a strong social fabric. The Yellins have provided us with an inheritance, carefully preserved and presented at just the right moment.

"It isn't much fun to be the friction that slows the machine," they write. Fun it may not be, but its legalities and logistics are very instructive. Among the things to savor in this telling—and there are many—is the profound detail of it.

In the Yellins' story, solidarity shines throughout. First is the affection and camaraderie between Jean and Ed themselves. The kind of sharing they do in this memoir can only come from years of thinking, working, cooking, cleaning, and—obviously—arguing together about how to bring about a better, more just world.

I spend my time organizing, teaching, and hanging out in the contemporary left. It is a heady, exciting place to be now. The people who power our social and political movements are mostly younger than I am (I'm in my early '40s). It is a magnificent thing to learn from the new ways they see the world, from the questions they ask that I have never considered, from the experiences they bring forth that show us a whole new political horizon. Theirs is a leadership we sorely need in this country.

Too many younger leftists have no idea what it's like to have our elders appreciate us and our work. So what a gift it is that the Yellins close their story with a hurrah for political candidates who are now running explicitly as socialists. I thank Ed and Jean for their fight, for their tenacity, for their piece of history—and for passing it on to us.

I often think about how my younger comrades have little experience with the actual humans of the Old Left. That's for obvious generational reasons, but not only those. It's because the right-wing repression so thoroughly cataloged in *In Contempt* drove so many people from the left. It's also because the New Left has its own story, emerging from its own material realities and enshrined in the media and the people most available to the media.

In Contempt is an important corrective—a tether to the organizing of the 1930s, '40s, and '50s, when the Yellins and thousands of their comrades made a mass movement with revolutionary goals for our society and our world. In their story is a strong length of social fabric that is almost impossible to imagine in our current conditions. You can pull its ends and see it snap, as Jean and Ed go back and forth in the text. Their clarity is remarkable, as are their commitment to one another and their political vision. It's clear from their account that their children, their siblings, and their comrades were necessary to their keeping that commitment. That, too, is a solidarity that gleams.

There are many people in this story, and the ones who stick out are the steadfast ones: playmates, neighbors, teachers, anonymous donors, Quakers who host weekly potluck dinners. It's their fierce holding on to one another that shines through—as does the unappreciated work of childcare and "so much typing," as Jean writes—and the camaraderie of communities full of unapologetically left, unapologetically secular Jews, practicing their own *l'dor v'dor* (generation-to-generation) solidarity in the Coops and the cities and the unions in which they found new ways to express our ancestral ethics.

Not since *Red Diapers*—published in 1998, when many of my comrades were little kids—have we had powerful first-person accounts of this far-reaching era, which continues to shape our own. In other stories—and it's important to read those, too—are the explanations of how the pressure of state repression on Marxist, Communist, Jewish, Black, and other communities exploded whatever latent dysfunctions existed inside and between people, destroying relationships, families, and movements. We see how even the pettiness of repression—those pencils from Johns

Hopkins!—gets conscripted into the pressure to break our politics. That, too, is familiar: When I worked for a union newspaper, we had to count column inches and report them in our federal paperwork. Antiworker, antijustice machinations are devious and specific, long-lasting, and enshrined.

That lesson, too, is important for our movements today. We seek to undo forty-plus years of neoliberalism, centuries of colonialism and racism, the ravaging of our planet, and, instead, institute, in the words of one contemporary comrade, "an irreversible shift in the balance of power and wealth in favor of working people." We must enshrine our victories in ways that make it much harder for our opponents to dismantle them, and easier for us to keep organizing for that which we know we need and also that which we can't predict.

In Contempt is a moving account of the Yellins' time weaving the old strands with the new. So much time and money has been spent in shredding their handiwork—and thank goodness it has not been wholly successful. We are so lucky that the Yellins and their comrades fabricated such a strong strand—tough enough to withstand the repression of the federal government, soft enough to cover a sleeping child—and that now, in their advanced years, have brought forth this record of their experience of how to do so. Let that also be our lesson, to place again the old threads with the new. We need to learn from the Yellins' tenacity to hold fast in the face of repression. Their telling of how to rely on and support one another, to push and to argue and to play together, is one that I'll return to as we—hopefully—build movements to shape this world around human needs and for human dignity, and to find the power to make those changes in priorities last.

—Dania Rajendra
Inaugural director, Athena Coalition